Escence

by

Monika Kispal

Copyright page

Part 1
Prelude

O friend unseen, unborn, unknown,
Student of our sweet English tongue,
Read out my words at night, alone
I was a poet, I was young.
Since I can never see your face,
And never shake you by the hand,
I send my soul through time and space
To greet you. You will understand.

James Elroy Flecker

To A Poet A Thousand Years Hence

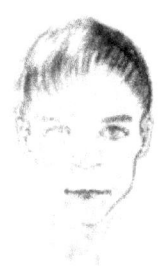

"You are trembling."

A young man, dressed in a short, dark blue cloak and brown trousers was leaning above a tallish boy in the mist of sea foam, searching the blurred vision of the boy's misplaced mind. The boy was shaking in his thick, light brown coat, his arms were out of place, rumbling around his body. He raised his arms to calm the movement.

"My boat... turned over...," his teeth were clattering in his mouth half open.

"What happened?" asked the other man, curiously.

"I don't know. I saw some kind of light... in me and around me...," he silenced. He was still standing above him, his arms stretching towards the boy's hands.

"Let me help you up. You could come with me... somewhere safe... where you can recover from this."

The boy nodded, he seemed to be struggling to talk.

"Which way?"

The young man raised his head towards the North. Then suddenly lowered his chin to his shoulder blade looking into the distance.

"I'll lead you."

He stepped forward in the wet sand. His weight sunk into it less and less as they were heading off the seashore. He was a very young man, in his early 20's. His short brown hair attached to a short forehead above a long nose. The mouth was reflecting the darkness of his coloured facial skin which had a tone of watery playfulness, most of which was concealed by his eyeglasses. It was hard to tell the emotions of this face, to say what age was easier: he was shining behind his dark complexion.

"What's your name?" the boy asked him.

"Fife."

"Fife? What kind of name is that?"

"An old one," said Fife laughing.

"Why are you laughing at me... you are not old at all, how old are you?"

"Hm...," he looked at the boy thinking, "I don't know... really, and you?"

"Well, I am seventeen, I think."

"You think... What's your name?"

"I can't recall," he stopped to breathe, the idea that he was not remembering his name pumped his heart running, "God almighty...," he was gasping for air.

Fife stopped, too, they had to take a short break so that the boy could calm down.

"You are wearing a military uniform; you must be a soldier. On a ship?"

"I can't remember... only the boat... turning over..."

They were walking up steep slopes of brownish grass filling up the horizon which ascended to a hillside far away.

"Where are you from?" the boy asked, recovering from his distress.

"The village."

"What village?"

"That one," he raised his arm to a blurred brown cloud in the distance, "I don't remember its name."

"Where are we going, then?"

"There is a cave behind those hills, I live there."

They were breathing in the late spring air of 1917. The field grass they were going through was curving under the cool breeze from the sea. It was sweet and light, mixing with the air of the warm day. It was blowing delicately, but the clouds in the cerulean light of the sky still seemed to be affected by the strong winds of past cold days in their floppy shapes and fluffy sideburns.

"The wind is nice today... no mistral or sirocco...I..."

"Mistral? Am I in France?" the boy asked Fife, astonished, "How come you speak English then?"

"You are wearing a British Military uniform."

The young man looked down to his clothes, a feeling of being wiped out struck him again.

"Amnesia," he said the word.

"Yes, you have amnesia. I think it would be best for you to have a couple of days of rest and we will see your memory return, I am sure," said Fife. He saw the boy was still seized by the experience of losing his memory.

"Do you know why the grass is brown?"

"No..."

"Look closer..."

"Oh my..." he says, "It is the sand... but just you wait, what is this? It is a hat!" he squatted to see what the object was.

"It's my hat!"

"What?"

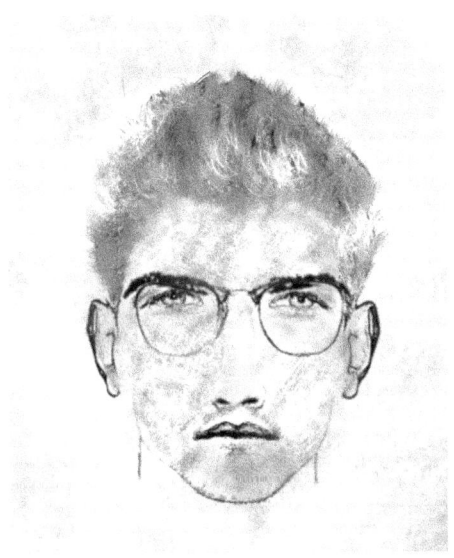

Fife

"It is my hat. How can it be so far from... my landing...?"

"An animal might have brought..."

"But there are no prints..." he cut into his words, his senses returning to reflex the question down.

"It looks like a British military hat... The wind?"

"No, no, you said no wind today, it is not that strong... and how could this be... so far away?"

"A bird? Who knows...? Do you know when you fell in the water at all?"

"I must not have spent much time in there... at least, I could have drowned..."

"Where were you, do you remember?"

"Well, I remember the waves, as I was swimming," said he hesitantly, "I think I saw this light, but it felt strange, it looked like it was somewhere under me... in the water," he was recollecting the memories of being in there, and suddenly he had to close his eyes, "Oh, it was... a shock... I do not remember..."

The thin skin on his face was even whiter than before, his short hair giving no shade or coloring to its fresh tints. His eyes were of kaleidoscopic confusion of browns and blacks, looking helpless at his company.

"Do not bother about it. You can have a rest in the cave, everything is going to be fine."

He got lost in his thoughts again, going forward without speaking towards the slanting horizon. They reached the cave after an hour's walk.

"Hah. Such an establishment," said the boy, smiling at the level of furbishing within the cave.

"I've always lived here. Take this blanket, I will build a fire later. So, what happened, tell me again?"

"I don't know. My boat turned over and then ... I don't remember. But I saw this light... in me, around me, everything went dark, then I felt this light in me... and then outside me, it was heavy and light at the same time..."

"Look at my hand when I touch you. Is this what you saw and felt?" said Fife, curiously. He put his hand on his elbow. A faint line of shimmering light up around their skins in the dark.

"What's happening? Yes, this is exactly what happened."

"I wanted to show you…, I did not build the fire so that you can see this. The same thing happened to me… ages ago. My boat turned over and I fell into the water. I also saw that light… so many years ago… "

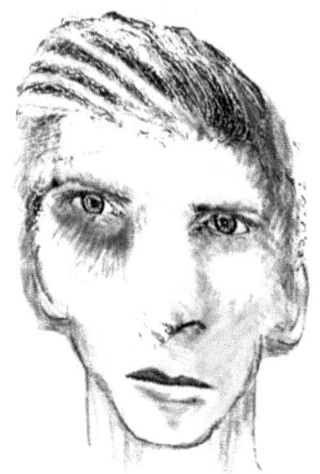

The ancient truant

The wind was howling from the sea. It helped the ancient truant in finding his way home through the forest. His senses sharpened, he was given the smell and coldness of direction by the wind. He was descending silently, scattering leaves with his feet. Going on. Rain-fresh stones. Blue ravine rocks. The darkness shines blue in the moss. Who are you, ancient truant? *Names sink into depths when one wanders the world for thousands of years: his name was Mof.*

He came up to a slope, which led him out of the ravine. The forest around him was loud and alive, no creature noticed his arrival. The sounds of his steps were lost under the feet of a hyena: he grew up in Angkor, in the company of the wild animals, born to a family of farmers and shepherds. His eyes reminded you of that of animals, looking intense and blunt at the same time. They saw everything and nothing: only what they had to see. His face under bore no lines, they were lost into the depths of a vibrant skin; still, the skin of the mouth was rigid.

He was heading for the entrance of a cave. The smell of fire opened his nostrils, flares of flames hit his eyes. He heard sounds from the distant depths of the cave. Two men were talking. Mof was waiting at the entrance for their conversation to end.

"Fife," Mof said, when they stopped talking.

"Mof, old friend, where have you been?" he said laughing. He had just realized that he was in the cave.

"Around. Who is your friend?"

"Well, do you remember?" Fife turned to the boy.

"I still can't remember...," he said slowly. He felt strange in the presence of Mof, whose face was ancient and young at the same time. He was not afraid of him, but Mof's powerful and queer outlines spooked him as if he was seeing a spectre. And still, he felt they had already known each other from a long time ago.

"Why is he here?" Mof asked Fife.

"I found him on the shore, in the water... he is... he has gone.... he saw the light...."

"Yes?" the shadows in Mof's eyes deepened with curiosity, "What happened?", he asked.

The young boy did not answer, he looked desperately at Fife.

"He suffers from amnesia," Fife explained to Mof.

Mof's eyebrows raised to signal his understanding. He sat down by the fire.

"You came a long way...," he was steering the boy's uniform, "On a ship?"

"I do not remember."

Mof sighed.

"You will know," he pulled Fife to the deeper parts of the cave. They started to talk, unheard. The boy could only catch a couple of words; "we did not have".

"Let's call you Four," Mof said, returning to the fire.

"Four?"

"Four. It is a number," answered Mof.

"But why a number?"

"Hell," Mof murmured, "You like something more *modern*?" uttering the word with unfamiliarity, "Where I come from, we used simple words to name. Bread. Three. Hyena."

"Your names? Where are you from?"

"Asia, Angkor."

"But you do not look at all like any Asian, you must have had a white family."

Mof looked at him for a long second.

"It is hard for me to understand your talking. Talk to me slower and use simple words."

"But why? Are you sick? You have amnesia?" he hoped he did not have to take in the words he formerly heard, "Why are you looking at me like that?"

"Hell, the way I look," Mof muffled impatiently, "I don't even see you..., I see through you. I am more than 6000 years old."

There was silence.

"I'll tell you things. You are the fourth person. So, I called you four," Mof spoke again.

"Fourth... in what line?"

"I was first. To meet the light."

"What I saw? Where?"

"In the water."

"What is it?"

"I don't know. Some kind of energy... when I fell in... 6000 years ago, it was this same light... "

"But what does it do to you?"

"One thing, you won't die. I could not and he could not." He stood up and stepped closer to Fife.

"How old are you?

Fife turned to the boy.

"I was a Roman soldier. Before Christ."

They did not speak for a while waiting for him, thinking.

"Who is the third man? Or woman? You said I was fourth."

"His name is Thee. Ha was born in Corsica. 1500. "

"And this light that was shining on our skins? When you touched my elbow?"

"Yes, that's a field of energy," Fife explained, "Well we have learned it changes when we are three. And now you are here..."

"So, what happens when we are three?"

Mof looked at Fife.

"It might hurt. He is vulnerable, with amnesia. Let's wait for Thee."

"Is he... around?" Four asked, "When is he coming?"

"We don't know. He traveled to Corsica because of the war. He has family members. "

"But he is 400. Has he got children?

"He looks after the descendants of his family, I mean. From a distance. He had no children," Fife interrupted.

"We could send him a telegram," Mof looked at Fife, nodding.

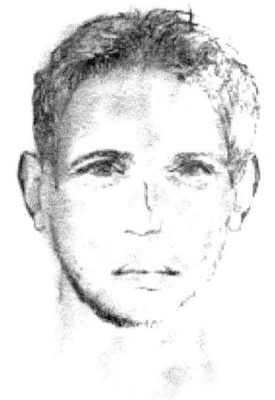

There was a sense of timelessness in their waiting; they had been waiting for a long time. Four sensed patience in their behavior, they switched back to a slow life after a couple of days. He sunk with them into this pace of living, which felt more and more natural. The hot French days were slowly darkening his skin and soul into a deep understanding of nothingness. The cobalt skyscapes of summer erased his wanting to remember or go home, his memory was still blank.

"Thee," said Mof one day, "You came back," seeing him entering the cave entrance.

"I got your telegram, so here I am."

Thee's shining face was smiling at Mof under that same effect of fluidity all the others had on their faces and bodies. His smile was almost wriggling under his nose. He brought darker skin tones from the harsher sunshine of Corsica. He blinked at Mof.

"How are you?"

"All right. We have found someone."

"Oh, that's why you wanted me here?"

"He didn't write it to you?"

"**Come as fast as you can. STOP.** I wasn't worried for you," he smiled.

"No need." Fife joined the conversation waking from his sleep on his bunk bed.

"What did you dream of?" Mof asked Fife, "Everyone was... in some kind of frenzied dreaming all night."

"Me as well," said Thee.

"I felt wanting to touch that light again," said Four getting out of bed, "I still feel it, so strong."

"Me too."

"And me."

"And I." repeated Mof, "There must be some meaning to this, now that we are four."

"Let's go back out to the sea today," said Mof, "I'll get the boat."

"We have the sea," said Mof, laughing at the others.

"You love the sea," Four turned to him.

"Who does not?" said Fife, "We all love it. That's why we are here."

"Seaman."

"Seaman."

"Seaman."

"Seaman."

They all started laughing.

"What if we create a circle and try what happens?" asked Four, who was all too curious about the effects of the light.

"In the boat? I don't think so. What about that rock?" said Fife, turning to the wheel. He pointed the boat at a large mass of rock in the distance.

"Do you know what kinetic energy is?" Fife turned to Four.

"No. I wasn't educated," Four said.

"You are not familiar with physics."

"No."

"Don't mind. You will learn. But, for now, I just say this light gives us a certain energy..."

"Like heat?" Four interrupted.

"Yes."

"So, what's this kinetic energy?"

"Well, kinetic means motion."

"The heavier you are, and the more your speed is, the more of this energy you will have," said Thee, frowning his eyebrows.

"Let's not confuse the kid for now. So, we get motion energy when we are three. The energy of your moving body is kinetic energy."

"Ok," said Four, "We are going to move. How?"

"We don't know yet. You haven't seen us three together yet. I can't think of what can happen when we are four."

"So, what happens when you are three?"

"It's a shaky feeling. Most of the time, I got sick," said Thee, "I wouldn't do it for fun."

Their boat arrived at the rock. They all got out.

"This spot feels just fine," said Fife, looking at them, "Let's just do this," he sighed.

"Holy…" Four was yelling, but his voice was lost in the whirlwind the touching of their hands created. A maelstrom of sea foam swallowed their bodies as small sparkles appeared in the air; they were moving forward in the burst of an energy field. As their hands lost touch in the confusion, they slowed down to be ejected onto the hard rocks of the small island.

"God almighty…" said Fife still hurling his hands from losing his balance, "This was…"

"This was crazy!" Four was shouting.

"I don't think we will try this again," said Mof later, getting back to their boat, "I wonder why we have this urge to go back. To dream back."

"We might never know," Thee laughed, "Might be some law of physics."

Sitting back in the boat they fell into silence. They were all exhausted because of what happened.

"I wonder what the future will be…" said Four later, still thinking about the maelstrom, "Do you think we could travel in time if we held hands long enough?"

"Why, I don't know," said Fife, "We will just have to wait for it."

Part 2

2155

The owl was clueless about the odd way the druid was speaking. It was not his words, though. It was the way he formed the words. There was an impediment in the druid's speech, but the owl could not guess why. *He was too young for a stroke and too old for a speech therapist.*

"The dream is always the same," said the druid in his soft and deep tones, "This dream must be divine to come to me every night at the very same hour, to fill me up with vision, when you friends, you lie in sandman's arms," he paused to breathe.

"I vision a marvellous tree before me, suspended in the golden air. The tree has the dark of the night – the branches hold the king in shadow and shelter, hiding him between mossy boughs. My kins, the talking stones inhabit the corners of the world, and the nails of my fingers glitter in the middle of the cross beam. The living force of winged bodies gather with bright eyes to guard the growth and thickening of the tree. My body is shamed in the light of their look - the triumphant tree hangs there – in the middle of the forest, and animals assemble without wings under the roots," here the druid paused again and looked around.

"I don't have half of my tongue, but I like to feel words. Please, forgive me for my speech," he said, "My name is Thornton."

The people he was talking to were sitting around a large fire pit. They were silent. Thornton examined his listeners with his deep brown eyes before he continued.

"I may sound hard to understand. Do you want me to explain my words?"

Nobody answered.

"Are you those young kids who I met under the cliffs?" he continued, directing his question to a group sitting separated, "I was talking about my dream vision."

"We have no idea what it is. Do you dream, or see something? Or do you hallucinate?" one lad asked.

"Have you ever had a dream...," started the druid, "I have a dream ... with every dawn, at the very same hour..."

One of the kids interrupted.

"How do you know it is the same hour?"

"It comes to me every morning at the very same hour... I know because I always wake from this dream with a sudden shiver... and then the sun, as I look at the sun in the east, is under that branch, where that owl is sitting."

"There's an owl, boys, really, I have never seen a real owl," the kid said.

The druid drew close to the fire.

"Will you have tea?" he asked, looking into an old cauldron.

"Don't you know? You have visions, or what," the lad talking sneered at him and got up from the ground, "My name is Drizzle. We met yesterday under the cliffs, you sent us to hell."

"Oh, yes, I remember you."

"We had to sleep here in the forest, 'cos our bikes were stolen."

"Your bikes? I did not see them. What make?"

"They were special mountain bikes, expensive. Six. We want them back. It's thirty miles back to Vertical. We can't hitch-hike, there's no motorway from this patch."

"We could help you find those bikes. I don't think they were stolen. I think you simply lost them. We did not see anyone else in the forest yesterday."

"You may be right," said a yellow-haired girl who was sitting next to the lad talking, "I told them we shouldn't leave the bikes there."

"Could you describe the place where you left the bikes? We know this forest very well."

"Phew. Trees. Leaves. Bushes. Roots. What else?"

"I mean you must have seen something noticeable where you left the bikes. Or somewhere near."

The kids were thinking in silence, but not one of them remembered anything.

"We will never find them," sighed the yellow-haired girl.

"What did you do when you put down your bikes?" the druid asked.

"We picked up the bags and walked. Drizzle has a POS system with him, but he forgot to bring solar."

"Was it working when you started?"

"I think not."

The druid sighed.

"If you have no idea where the bikes are, we can search in twos later. It is too cold now. Did you sleep around the fire?"

"Yes, fortunately, Gabe saw the fire last night."

"I tell you what. We'll check every place where you could have left them. Hopefully, we will find them soon and you can ride home in the afternoon."

The kids looked at him with grateful eyes. They started to talk about where they would find the bikes, which way they should go, and the yellow-haired girl drew a map with the help of a man whose name was Kurtz. He was a strange man, staring with his blurred eyes from under his glasses. The glasses were special and not conspicuous at all. They recorded, they protected. His face was not old, but the glasses fooled the viewer into thinking him to be.

"I know the forest very well," Kurtz said, "I have been living here for thirty years. It is a vast forest, but I don't think you could get too far, eh?" he nodded.

"I think we walked two hours back from the cliffs after we met him. We did not really move after sunset."

"Seems you were moving in a curve by these paths," Kurtz said and drawing a line on his map with his gloved left hand, "The cliffs are about six or seven miles away."

"Yes, we always followed the paths to the cliffs," said the yellow-haired girl, "Why are you living here?"

Kurtz did not answer her question. He sunk into his thoughts drawing more lines. The yellow-haired girl took no notice of his silence.

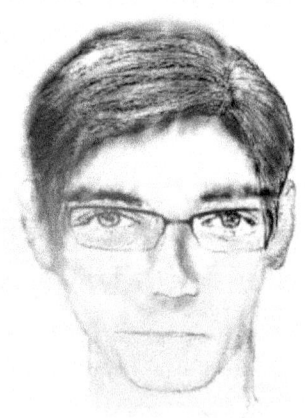

"Who is that girl by his side? Why is she here? Why does she live here?"

"She is Alex, she had lived here alone, but she moved in with the druid, because she feared being alone. She told me when she first slept here, she tied herself to this tree, on a higher branch," said Kurtz pointing at the owl sitting on the branch, "If you go east, you will find a small house on a big one."

"You mean a tree?"

"The druid lived there for six years, but it was ruined in a gale, and he had to come down, the monkey," Kurtz was smiling, "Animals and insects are dangerous in the dark," said the yellow-haired girl.

"Birds are not. These birds attack in daylight," Kurtz laughed at her silently.

"Attack?" she screeched.

"Not here, this is deep forest, but they rule the cliffs. Once a raven attacked me from the cliffs you wanted to climb yesterday. They are territorial, almost all of them. And dangerous in their own ways."

"Why, why do you live here? You could live in Vertical? Anyway, we often come here to climb, but not in the forest."

"I chose this place to live a long time ago... It is a beautiful place." Kurtz was winking in the harsh morning sun.

"Is it? I think this place sucks."

"Why, are you bored?"

"We just came here to climb."

"That's where you met the druid?"

"Yes, he tried to put us off, there was some nesting restriction."

"And your friends?"

"Drizzle? It is a power sport for him. He climbs with plugs, because he is bored."

"That's dangerous. Why don't you climb indoors rather than coming here?" Kurtz looked at her curiously, "Isn't this place far?"

"At first, we were cycling in the forest, but we started to go faster and deeper, and then we found the cliffs. There weren't any owls there."

"Not now that they are nesting."

Thornton came back to their conversation; he spoke loudly, he wanted everyone to hear.

"Do you have headlights? If you have, it is best to take them with you, all of you. If we lose you, we will see you in the dark."

"Do you want to make the search into the night?" asked Kurtz laughing.

"I don't think it will be necessary, just in case.

The sun was on the opposite side of the tree when they returned.

"We will find them tomorrow," sighed the yellow-haired girl.

"We need to extend the search and must go further down to the cliffs. You will need to walk a little bit longer tomorrow and be more careful. One of you must stay close to the path," said Kurtz, leaving them to lie around the fire.

"I badly bruised myself when I opened that tap to fill the bathtub," the yellow-haired girl said suddenly, scratching her elbow.

"Why, don't you have wired bathrooms?" Drizzle asked, surprised.

"We do not have one, actually," she said, "My father just hates it. We have no electricity in the house."

"Phew. It is... strange. What do you do in the dark?"

"I have old parents and they like it. They screw in the dark."

"People fear old, wired homes," said Drizzle.

"Why?"

"The *Silkwire* is full of those shit accidents in the bathrooms and kitchens. Did you see that story about that man in Rye? The emergency unit was literally re-configured as a permanent presidential suite. Ever."

"Wow. Why?"

"Shocked and hit the bottom."

"It does not happen often, Drizzle. Rye is an ancient town."

"It's always an accident; those systems don't work well in old houses. They can't insulate what they install. They do not have accidents in the skyscrapers," said the yellow-haired girl.

"Gabe, can I ask you a question?" said Drizzle after a quiet minute.

She leered at him.

"I am in love with an imaginary ornithologist," she said, leering at him.

The yellow-haired girl guffawed.

"I always had an imaginary dragonfly with me when I was a kid," Gabe said, "I've always found it interesting how to believe in imaginary things. Don't you, Drizzle, you are gamers aren't you?

"That's different. I know I am not there."

"Don't lie, bastard. You have just told me you have to come back when you are out," said the yellow-haired girl.

"It wouldn't work if I... but it doesn't last long," Drizzle said "For six hours...he-he."

A pellet the owl belched up landed on Drizzle's forehead. He woke up and shook his head. The yellow-haired girl woke up next to him.

"I had a dream, Drizz," she said, yawning.

"Don't dream."

"I don't often have dreams."

"I almost always dream and always have some shit dream. You are lucky."

"I think I would like to dream more," she said, yawning again.

"There are some interesting techniques you can use to make yourself dream. I think it's very easy. You can induce a dream," said Gabe, woken from his sleep by their conversation, "There's this urine induced dream. You have to drink too much or be very thirsty."

"And?"

"If you drink too much, you will have dreams about going to the loo, or something. I remember when we went to that ski camp last year, I drank too much, and it was hot, and I dreamt that I sat in the fridge and couldn't pee."

"Weird."

"I have to pee," Gabe got up from the covers Thornton gave him last night and hid among the trees.

"She doesn't think it's real," said the yellow-haired girl to Drizzle, giving a dark look to her leaving figure.

"She is nuts."

"She thinks it ... it's something like a tool for her ... she knows it doesn't exist. She made it up 'cos she was alone, and she thinks it helps her think about things she can't control. I mean she can talk about these things at least... she uses it to talk about things she couldn't."

"I don't think she is OK. And that dragonfly?" Drizzle hawked.

"Why don't you try it, Drizzle?" said the yellow-haired girl giggling.

"What do you mean? Imagine something? Shut up."

They were sleeping again when Thornton came back later. They divided the territory into ten squares and decided to rake the forest up to the cliffs. Thornton and Alex were following the creek to the cliffs. Thornton took his shoes off and waded into the cold water.

"It is so hot, won't you come in, I can't keep your pace."

She took off her shoes.

"This creek is so cold, why don't you get the cramp?" she laughed.

"I must be the devil himself," he laughed, "What do you think of them? And Drizzle? He is hostile."

"He is a teenage gamer; how could he understand you? Yesterday we were out together. He saw nothing. He literally has no side vision."

"We could help him."

"How?" Alex sighed and patted the druid on the shoulder.

"I'll try to talk to him."

They followed the creek till the spring.

"When I hear this creek gurgle, I feel that something is happening," said the druid when they arrived, "I cannot get bored of it."

"When you are with me, I feel the same."

"I know," said the druid, "We should hurry. It is getting dark. Get me out of here," he stretched his hand to touch her fingers.

"You are really low," she said, laughing.

Gabe and Kurtz found the bikes at last, hidden under thick foliage.

"I'll pull a string to the path and come back for the rest of the bikes. We will take two now," said Kurtz.

"I don't remember this place," said Gabe.

"It seems you hid them very carefully here; it is strange you can't remember."

"I remember putting the bikes down, but nothing else."

"You must have been listening to music."

"I don't think I would remember this anyway. I mean there is nothing to remember. This place was hidden."

"Do you know these trees?"

"We have not been introduced," she said laughing.

"OK, you don't know them by the name, but you can remember the smell of the trees, the shape of the letters, the shape of the roots, the color of the bark. Do you know what they are doing now?"

"Oh, they are doing something?"

"Apart from growing really very slowly," said he, looking at the smallest one, "They take in air, emit air, and photosynthesize, and..."

"I know this from school."

"You breathe in directly what they breathe out, oxygen. Otherwise, it is higher up. What do you know from school?" said Kurtz slightly sarcastically, "I had a bad pneumonia a long time ago, it did not want to heal. When the weather got colder, I felt like sleeping under willow trees every night. The trees had a cold stress and threw off methyl salicylate. It cured my lungs in two weeks. The pills I bought did not help... They use this chemical to make aspirin. These trees use it to talk to each other. Hey, here's the guy who kicked you last night, says this birch and the other will trip you up. They really can be angry." he said, mockingly.

"You are kidding. It's in a horror movie."

"Yes, I was kidding. But it's funny, isn't it? An angry tree cured me."

"Funny."

They returned all the bikes to the fire. The kids were packing up, shouting enthusiastically to each other, but could only set out on the following day, so they settled down to sleep again.

The owl was eating a mouse quite enthusiastically on the tree in the moonlight.

"I thought only vultures do this," said Drizzle, "I need to throw up."

"They eat anything when they are hungry, ravens, eagles, small birds, they all do. There is not much food in the forest, you know," said Kurtz.

"What do you eat?"

"Mushrooms. Pine nuts, berries."

Kurtz left the kids under the tree alone.

"It may be your mushrooms," said Drizzle mockingly. He was sitting right under the owl now, and they started to talk about Alex. Drizzle listened in silence, but something came to his mind.

"You're not gonna believe this! We went out together on the first day. She sat by the riverbank singing, and some eel-like something was standing out there half his body out of water for an hour," said he in his hoarse voice, "Nuts."

"You find her very interesting?" asked Thornton, who overheard the conversation in the dark, coming to the fire with her.

"She is..., she is a very precious friend."

"Very precious, indeed," said Kurtz, who returned to the fire in the footsteps of the druid, "I heard you were really bored here."

"Why, what about this eel, do you really believe that it was listening to her song?" asked Drizzle.

"I do not know, Drizzle," said Kurtz, "There is one thing I can know, that I cannot know what was happening."

"I am sure there must be some scientific reason, you had that tree story. It was scientific," said Gabe to Kurtz, yawning.

"Yes, I think, there may be," grumbled he, "Look, it is never that easy, even if there is, even if we look at it very, very rationally and scientifically, even then ... I mean everything works according to some logic, and we can even know that, but how will you know the reason ... I mean there may be... some other reason that you could never think of."

"You're a stupid old man," said Drizzle, "It must be some brain trick."

"Really? Brain trick?" shouted the druid, "Do you really think you can be this clever to understand everything? Don't you think this whole thing around us is too... big to understand... I mean we see, see things around us, but we always see what we can, and what we want or what really...," he was drifting into a long and angry philosophical explanation, but Kurtz stopped him.

"Hey, Thornton, we are hungry. What's for supper?" said he, tapping his watch.

"Tea is ready, and we still have some mutton to stew, from the forester," said Alex.

"That should be enough for us. When was he here?"

"Four days ago. You were not lucky," said Alex to the kids, "He could have taken you back to Vertical."

"We wanted to find the bikes, anyway," said the yellow-haired girl.

"It is all right," added Drizzle, "I think I grew a little tired of gaming."

"I see. Alex said something... about your mind," said Thornton.

Drizzle looked at him suspiciously.

"It is about the way you are using your brain. Your brain normally uses all the senses to determine reality. It is not only your eyes. Your ears, the smells, and your skin are all used to see what is around you. It stops working normally if you play too much. You are almost always watching in one direction, and when you look sideways, you always turn your head. Like that owl," said Thornton pointing at the bird, "You see, she has a very subtle mind ... who would notice this?"

"You really game too much, young man," Kurtz was leering at the owl.

"Yeah, I know, I've just told you. What's this fuss about, after all these games help me to..." He fell into silence.

"To?" They all turned their heads to hear his answer.

"It's my stupid imagination. I just switch it off and play."

"What's the matter with your imagination?" asked Kurtz.

"It's not that I hallucinate or have visions. It's just ... sometimes I think of things ... I shouldn't ... I mean what makes you fear," answered he slowly.

"I think you can learn to control it," said Kurtz.

"You are sick, not your imagination," said the yellow-haired girl.

"If you have no imagination, you cannot conjure any one single idea about this world," said Kurtz, "You will not understand what is happening to you; if you only use your senses, you are a machine. Imagination helps you to build a world from the senses, to build your past, present and future. You can see it in your head, and you can hear it inside your head," he smiled "Imagination will build memories for you. And it is not only to see the past and the present, but the future. You will not simply be able to think of the future, but you can figure out what will happen. Eh?"

Drizzle became impatient with Kurtz's speech.

"All crap. This place is nothing. What the hell are you doing here? Is this your future? You can do nothing here. You do nothing here," said he.

"It really is fateful that we were here to help you," said Kurtz sadly.

"You know how I became a druid here?" Thornton cried, "These stones mean the world for me -, this is my world. I lost my tongue when my mother married again. I was five, and I was often beaten. Sometimes when we were alone it was very bad, I could not avoid the moods, I was often yelled at and bloody hit. When I was very young, I was frightened too much and did not dare to speak, but one day I could not stand and spoke out, and he told me to put my tongue between my teeth, and he hit me on the head and the half of my tongue I just bit off. But after that I lived in fear because my mother never divorced again. When I became sixteen, everything changed. I moved here. This man lived here, and I stayed with him, and he taught me everything he knew."

"I don't mind your crap. You are such bloody losers..."

Kurtz eyebrows shrunk into an angry expression.

"You are being stupid, Drizzle. You make him very sad," the yellow-haired girl looked at Thornton. Drizzle, with an arrogant shrug, turned away. The druid stood up and plunged among the trees, crying.

Later around the fire the kids were chatting as usual.

"I don't know, I was really slow somehow," Gabe said, "My first boyfriend left because I did not want to kiss him."

"How old were you?" asked the yellow-haired girl.

"Twelve," she said, "The second broke up 'cos I did not want to screw," she laughed.

"And what happened to your dragonfly?" asked Drizzle.

She dived into her bag and a dragonfly toy appeared in her hands.

"I always keep him with myself," she said, "But the other one, in my head, is imaginary."

"Imaginary or not, your problem is that you have never met anyone who you could really talk to," said the yellow-haired girl, "I mean that's what you use this dragonfly for, someone to talk to."

Long silence ensued their conversation. They were listening to the humming sprawling from the forest.

"Is that some ordinary owl?" asked Gabe, "I mean, I know owls are protected...but it's not a simple barn owl, is it?"

"B-a-r-n owl? I don't know, Kurtz is not here," said Drizzle, "You could ask him later."

"It is not ordinary 'cos you don't often see it. So, it's Mag Iiiiiiiiiiiiii C," said Gabe giggling.

Drizzle let out a sleepy *ass* under his covers, and they all fell asleep.

The next morning the kids packed up and left the fire on their bikes early in the morning. Alex and Kurtz were worried about the half-tongue. The forester brought bad news to the fire. He found the footprints near a precipice, and there were no signs of his coming down. They tried to find the body a few days later, but they found nothing. Kurtz and Alex found runes under an elm tree some days later. They were very embarrassed.

"Friends," said Alex, "They say your friends become mountains when they die."

"I don't know, Alex, you should not give up hope. There's no body," answered Kurtz, thinking.

"I want to find him, he may have hidden somewhere," she said, "I do not know what he can do in the dark..."

"An old ... er ... friend of mine used to say *Hope as grasshoppers do*," said Kurtz to Alex patting her knees, "We will find him."

Part 3

Vertical

"I am no bird; and no net ensnares me: I am a free human being with an independent will."

Charlotte Brontë, Jane Eyre

The vertical complex lined above old townhouses. The skyline was filled with skyscrapers above the old ones in the omnipresent blurriness of the towers' own reflections. Anywhere you went you couldn't see the end. Not with the eye. Fifty years ago, when the Asian continent drew its last breath, the United Nations decided to accommodate the population in newly built skyscrapers. The old buildings in town only meant boundaries on the maps; the tall ones filled up everything in the unseen structure of an endless hive. This you could see from above. And small and bigger spots of green.

The governing principle of how Vertical was built was based on the structural need to accommodate the towers for the satellite systems. Towering spikes connected systems in the joints. The old fiber networks they used before satellites lay unused. Now it was satellites only, floating bitwires to each square inch in Vertical. People could be seen from above. One could join this system, Silkwire, from anywhere. Signaling, In Low Correlation. Trillions of data flowing continuously, flooding the spikes with radio and microwave signals.

The old townhouses were also joined to these information systems. The electrical wiring in the old houses were different though, scrambling through clumsily old flesh of bricks and mortar.

Empty. Kurtz was going down deserted streets, empty of crowds and empty of aggression. Shop windows were popping up here and there without doors, only to serve in the minuteness of a second. These windows were serving fast, whatever you wanted from a set list of products and services.

Kurtz was astonished by the changes. And the cleanliness of the streets as he was walking towards Arbor Harbor.

He was on his way to meet the four people to whom he would always belong. They were four other people, four like him, with that special genetic combination to be able to host the virus that lived under the cover of waves in a warm bay of the Mediterranean Sea.

They have never left each other before for a long time. They always knew about each other. When Kurtz moved to the forest thirty years ago to be able to continue with the heterotroph experiments, they lost connection.

He stopped to pick up a large sheet of paper from the chromatic surface of the road, whose presence peaked out of the shining metallic structure. The roads were designed to gulp in any type of rubbish, from any source. But this piece of paper was surviving between the two hourly cleaning cycles. The skyscrapers and the towers would not allow for rubbish to run free in the air, the tall buildings were not hermetically sealed entities. They were living villages. Treesides and chickens living between generators.

The towers needed air to cool the processing of trillions of gigabytes of information. Rubbish in the air was a burden on the ventilation system of the Vertical complex.

Wired. They chose this name for the section of the complex above this Old city. A road separated the Old city from a patch of green; he was following up along this to reach his destination, Arbor Harbor. Satellites were following him, his every step, like everyone else's every step on the planet. SATIN was its name, a full system developed to see the people of earth, towns, and the complex throughout the day and the night falling on it.

They did not move away from earth. The rockets of history were resting in silos, and the aircrafts to leave earth for journeys in the previous century lay dormant under the brown covers of the United Nations. There was a secret behind this, what Kurtz knew too well. The satellites and their oscillation project: humans were not meant to leave. They could not. But even this was a secret people did not know.

And yet, despite his profound knowledge of this world, Kurtz was astonished deeply by the changes he faced after thirty years of absence. The shops, the surfaces, the shining were all too different.

An old memory of a restaurant came up in his mind. He was climbing up stairs towards this place he wanted to see, thinking he would not find it as it was before, but still hoping. *Everything has changed in the streets: new metal covering for the road and fluid plastic feeling for the houses. They bore their old faces, but not their old skin.*

He heard human voices as he was coming around the corner, and that special, low humming he remembered. The restaurant called **"NOSTALGIE"** was there, covered in that new plastic feeling. He entered, to calm his hunger and curiosity.

Kurtz was impressed by the new look of the building he was standing in front of; he stopped for a moment, nothing like he remembered from thirty years back. Still, that old building, the old structure, the old little figurines. 800 years of bricks, mortar and renovation. Covered in that thin innovative plastic material protecting the buildings. The sophisticated artwork still shone through the grayness it caused. The building was lit in certain parts, something close to the fluorescence of a greenish glow. Most of the imps were looking at you with a dark green fury of this same light, their pitch-black shadows moving in the background.

"He must have used the Escence, somehow," he murmured to himself as he was entering through an old brown wooden door.

Tall and thin shadowy phantoms were coming and going in the settling darkness of the falling sun. Entering the building and leaving without talking, or showing any signs of who they are or why they are there.

Kurtz noticed Fife in the corner of the hall; he was listening to the speaker on an ad-hoc pulpit.

He was standing there on his own, the other three were not there. Kurtz gave a signal to him with his left hand- two fingers crossed in the air, waiting for an answer from Fife's eyes. Fife soon realized the signal and his eyes soon discovered the face in the crowd, belonging to the whiteness of those fingers. He started to move towards Kurtz.

"Heeeeey," they hugged each other, "I haven't seen you... for thirty years?"

"Long time," Kurtz was smiling under a very small drop of water from his left eye," Where are the others?"

"Here and there, but everyone is around, in Arbor, I mean except you." Fife pulled him to a corner without people. Kurtz was talking.

"Oh, all right. I came to see you... because I need your help."

"Yes?" Fife answered in a curious tone.

"I want to find someone, and I need your help to find him. He disappeared without a trace. I think we would be able to find him... together. There were things that made me think that he could have been flicked to somewhere, we have already been."

"Where?"

"The owl's land."

"The owl's land. Was the owl there?"

"Yes, I saw it... but we did not talk. There were some kids lost in the forest, and I... could not."

"Oh. So, one of those kids is gone? They must be wired; it is easy to pick them on the Silkwire."

"Hell, no they have gone back to the vertical complex, but the other kid, this druid, ... probably he is wired though," he muttered, "But I'd have no idea how to find him, and as I told you I think he is with the owl."

"I know some guys who can give it a try.

"Will we need to **travel**?" He sounded the word strangely enough for Kurtz to understand what he meant.

"Yes, I'll drive," he said laughing, "I did not expect this... these changes..." he became gloomy in his tones, "I saw you such a long time ago. I missed you and I have just realized it now. Where are the others?"

"Hey, Mof lives in a small green barrack on the other side of the Harbor, Thee and Four have an old house. I run this kitchenpub and live here."

"Food for the people." Kurtz looked at him remembering his custom.

"Yes, free and paying customers. Obesity qualifies for payment," he started to laugh.

"Can I have a beer?"

"We have not had beer, I mean real beer for a time, only essentials now in circulation. Too many people. The skyscrapers provide almost everything. Green stuff, but only just enough. We need everything to eat. Nothing gets rotten or fermented."

"What's the situation otherwise?"

Twenty

"Let's go to Mof's place first. We can talk there..."

"Can you leave the kitchen... now, or do you need to close the place?"

"I have my managers; I don't have to worry," he peaked over Kurtz's shoulder to the counter area, "Hey Frank," he nodded towards a tall dark figure behind the counter, "I am leaving for tonight, close the hall without me."

He pulled Kurtz out of the hall through an old carved door to an alley.

"They have introduced birth control systems and inhibitors ten years ago, the population grows much slower now, we are down to around twenty billion."

"Twenty?" asked Kurtz back, astonished. "That's three billion down from twenty-three. They will not need the buildings... what is going to happen to all that..."

"Most of it will be pulled down at some point, the surrounding coastal areas are the most affected. The abandoned buildings are hard to handle, to wire as well, it's just load for nothing. Say they could use it to produce extra food, but the toxic waste is too much... we can't overeat."

Kurtz fell into the silence of thinking.

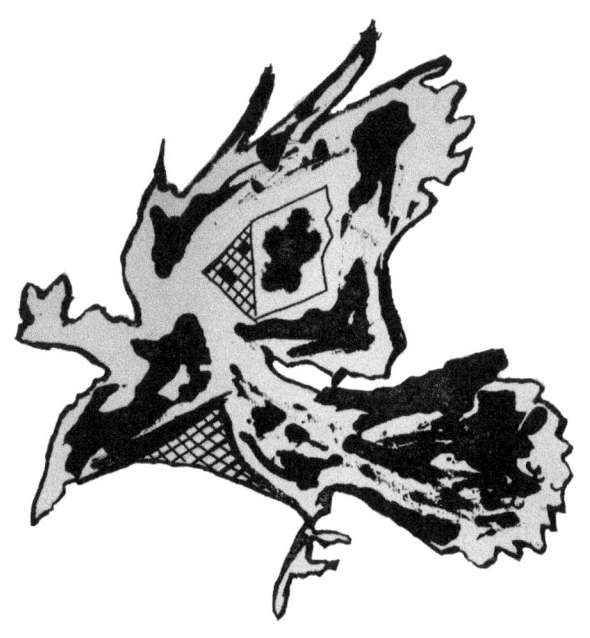

Mof was sitting in front of his green barrack, a wooden carved bench was peeking from behind his back - he was watching the surface of the water in the riverflow, rippling almost perfectly symmetrical. He had sadness in his eyes, looking at the crows.

"Black feathers. Angrier and angrier every day," he murmured to himself.

"Hey Mof," said Thee to wake him from his brooding.

"Hey, you," Mof realized Kurtz was among them, his eyebrows curling back to a calm expression, "Hey Kurtz, you are back."

"I missed you so much," answered Kurtz, "How are you?"

"I live under this barrack, there is a cave. Trees grow too straight for me outside."

"Let's go down?"

"So, what is this thing, what have you discovered?"

"I had a small laboratory in the forest, special microscopes. I have been watching the virus for many years. Yeah, I found out quite a lot."

"So?" They all looked at him with curiosity in their eyes.

"So, as you all know I went away to experiment with the colonies."

"What colonies?"

"I might... have not told you this... before, but you already know that there is a virus that lives in us, since we all had that encounter, so, it is not the Escence that keeps us alive or gives us the things we experience..."

"Then what?"

"It is the virus. To be exact, the virus colonies. As you were not around, I could only test my own colony, but I had experiments before."

"That herbivore thing?" asked Mof.

"Yeah, that. So, as I told you there is a colony of viruses living in us. After being infected by the virus, which then reproduces in large numbers..."

"Does this thing have anything to do with my amnesia?" asked Four, who never gained his knowledge back about his life again.

"Might have. But as I said, this virus keeps us alive. It's the colony that has survived, in you, the host for thousands of years."

"Why? And why us? Why not everybody else?"

"It's genetic."

"And my amnesia?"

"That, I don't know yet," he smiled at him," I went back as you did, so many times, but could not find out yet. Might be a simple fact of physics, though," he shook his head.

"You know, when we went back to that place, in 1917, when I... fell in, we never found it again."

"So what were the results of your experiments?"

"I discovered a way to see how the colonies interact in practice, when we are together. But that was too strong, to be examined... I mean when we are together."

"But you could control it with your devices. We were traveling."

"I left because I wanted to know how the virus is able to create this effect."

"And?"

"So, it turned out that the virus has a communication system that is sophisticated and evolving, as well. And evolving within a community. Their life is like a pyramid you know from the food chain."

"You mean they eat each other?" Thee grunted.

"Yeah. You could think of a colony, living in one of us, as heterotroph, living on energy your cells emit. But we all had this same type of colony in us. Things change when they get close. They create two chains, one is still heterotroph, and the second generation is herbivore, as they say."

"Virus eats virus?"

"Probably it is because they do not communicate with each other from two bodies, only in one. So, the viruses start eating each other, but it is also a process of evolution of information. They grow and they produce a new type of energy. The glow."

"Would this all mean that they were also affected by that light? Normal viruses don't work out like that," asked Thee, who was slowly catching up with the conversation.

"Yeah, that's what we suspect."

"Is that why we live long?"

"What I concluded within the experiments is that when you are infected, the virus keeps you young, fights cancer..., it wants to survive in you so hard it opens a new gate for you...to new worlds. Those living in you have learned to live with your human body through their evolution as well. They constantly learn and..."

"Evolve," Four finished the sentence, "Because of Escence?"

"That's where you caught the virus. But only a certain genetic combination will be affected like with normal viruses."

"So, what about that other... man? Is he also infected?" Fife wanted to know more about who they were looking for.

"Oh, no. He is... something else... in this story."

"Hm?"

The pamphlet

"Oh yeah, I've forgotten about this... What is this?"
Kurtz dug for the paper he found in the street.
"What is happening?" Fife took the paper from his hands to read it.

<!-- wp:paragraph -->
"Satin is about information 🛈 about money. It is there u just don't see it 🤐 or we all do now.
<!-- /wp:paragraph -->

<!-- wp:paragraph -->

Ppl don't like to be controlled. It has been poisoned from the very early stages. From within and without. By now they have sophisticated tricks. And I know how? I had a control friend. He does not believe in it 😵 it is rather impossible to control 20 billion ppl....it's got focuses of interest.
<!-- /wp:paragraph -->

<!-- wp:paragraph -->
Ppl started to think about it as a source of income after a while. They were after rich ppl. Then they rethought the whole thing and fought against it. Then they were after sensitive ppl. Back in the beginning it was too interesting, then too dirty, then... They grew bored even of that, the lies, the truth, their own flesh and blood.

<!-- /wp:paragraph -->

<!-- wp:paragraph -->
The number of satellites in the sky is approximately 5 times as official, last time your neighbor hacked it, it was above your head.
<!-- /wp:paragraph -->

You are doing it because you think ppl have to learn that they can be treated like this, on the same level, now their friends pick you... with hidden powers and hidden phrases... but how would you prove it without technology? I can't. This was all going towards to work people out of control, over their lives and senses... on that very reason of ...
<!-- /wp:paragraph -->

Will you listen to us?
Come to Arbor Harbor 2300, next Tuesday from now.

Fife nodded.

"You'll see. We could go to the Harbor now. It will be on in my place. But I must have received the message about your friend in the meantime."

"No. The kid is more important. You can tell me later."

"Not found," said Fife, reading out results from a sleek slice of print.

"So, is that the bitgun you'll use to find him?" asked Four.

"Hell, no."

"Were you using data?" Kurtz looked at Fife.

"Yeah. Did you go to Nostalgie?"

"Yes, I did," Kurtz answered, nodding.

"Did you see the images?"

"On the wall? Some."

"Why do we need it anyway? Why would we need to store the biodata of 20 million people? Why is this important? And every day?"

"This is not about size, anyway," said Kurtz evasively, avoiding to give reasons, even if he knew, "The idea is not in size," he repeated, "It is a matrix storage."

"They want it small."

"Small, yes. They store quite a lot of data."

"What do you mean it is not about the size then?"

"I mean they don't need to go down to atomic level, maybe nanotechnology. For storage. Or something newer. They were trying to store information on molecular and atomic level, but they realized they didn't need it."

"How then?"

"We stored data sequentially earlier, most often in bits. But you can store it in hexadecimal for example and create symbols to write them. It is much less load of data."

"Did they find the most optimal number system?"

"They don't have to. Not yet," Kurtz added, "If efficiency is your watchword, well that's e, I mean that's god's number to work with, but we don't need it. We only had to find *the better efficiency number* that works for us. The better efficiency for our needs."

"What's God's number?" Four cut in.

"The most optimal base system to store data. It is a non-integer base of numeration," Kurtz looked at him laughing.

"Oh, that," Four was scratching his head.

"So, that, we don't need it. We only need hexa and that needs sixteen symbols to store one day of twenty billion people on this small chip."

"Vitals?"

"Hell no," said Kurtz laughing, "They can't even..." he stopped talking because an object appeared in Fife's hand from his pocket, "read it consistently," he continued, "Now where did you get that? That's ancient."

"Is this a bitgun?"

"That's ancient," he repeated, "It is old stuff."

He switched it on when Fife put it in his hands.

"What can I use it for?" Kurtz ignored his question while playing with the buttons on the gun. It was flashing in blue and green lights.

"Is this the Escence?" asked Four, looking into the light.

"Is this the Escence?" repeated the question Fife, hearing no answer, "Judging by the color of flashing, it is," he added.

"Well, yes..." Kurtz murmured, raising one eyebrow, "I suspect you already opened this up."

"Yes, we used this tech to light up the buildings," Fife giggled.

"I was thinking what you could have used but had no idea that you had this... bitgun. It is ancient."

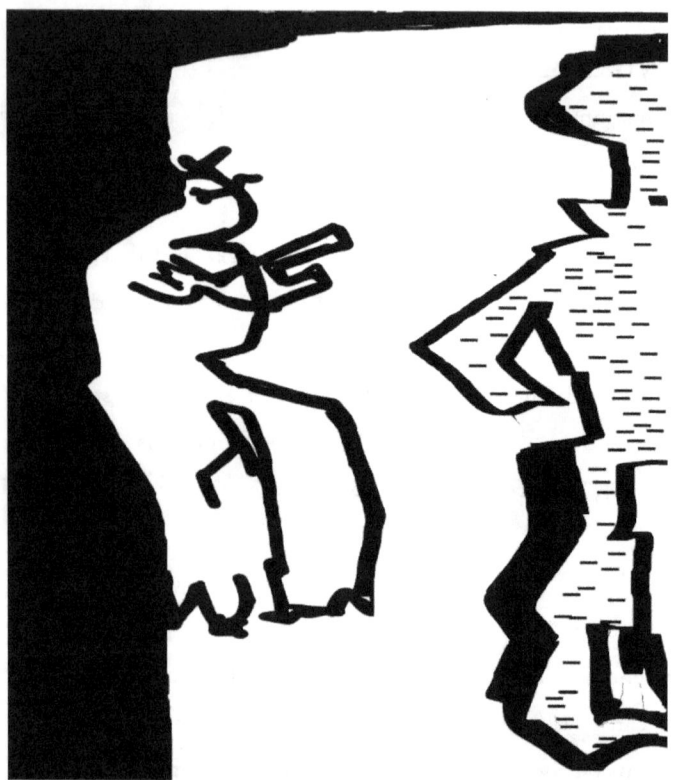

"We copied the small green gen inside."

"Not 3D. You have atom?"

"The 3D printer would not have been enough to print this, but you know this... You designed this?"

"Yes. And you need the atom printer to achieve that same effect. It only works on that subatomic level, the distinct energy fields of the electrons control the mechanism," he silenced for a second, before his mind pushed up a new question to be answered, "Where did you get the atom printer?"

"Aha, you are curious," said Thee laughing.

"Things have changed a lot since you have left... twenty years into overpopulating this globe, they can't follow people they used to. You know it is not the staff. It is the principle principle."

"The principle principle? What do you mean?"

"I think that skunk who coined it wanted, those graffitis still exist that spread the idea..." started Four.

"Skunk?" Kurtz interrupted him.

"Man. A person, I mean. So the man was spraying the walls and hacking everything he could to spread the idea," he did not go on, Kurtz raised his finger to stop him.

"The principle principle?"

"I think he wanted to say that it's his principle to have principles. What they started to forget about, again."

"Ah," said Kurtz, falling into silence, "Hey, it is not about being watched anymore, anyway."

"Man, you don't know. You were not here. You knew the old rules and you were working for a secretive agency, with the guns on that side. It's nothing like that now."

"You mean no agencies?"

"Well, obviously, we have them, but they function to supervise an automated system. Break-ins, hackings. I don't say they are capable of it. Just see that," he said, steadying his eyes on the bitgun, "Someone sold it to me. For food. This whole situation... they had to change everything. We don't have things we had before. I don't say I am missing them. Well, some," he looked at Kurtz thinking, "Did you go to Nostalgie?"

"Yes, I did, as I said."

"You saw those images then."

"Yeah, that was load from fifty years back. I said I saw the images," Kurtz shrugged, "There is, I mean there was strong support for those... at that time. Safety, security."

"And now?"

"Hey I don't know. You should know better," he looked at Fife relieved, his eyes smiling, "We must know better."

"After they built out those wide range sat systems, and people were abusing it, internally or breaking in... what they could see. They needed the bitguns because the UN introduced privacy protocols on a full scale, not partial then before," Fife's voice was fading away.

"Hmm," said Kurtz thinking, "It is getting very late. Can we go now? I need to find that kid."

Part 4

The tower

If everything that exists has a place, place too will have a place, and so on ad infinitum.

Aristotle: *Physics*

"This land is my homeland. In my mother tongue its name is *The Holy Land of the Holy Screech*. My name is Arethusa," the owl said to Half-Tongue, who was looking out of the window of a tower.

"What happened to my friends and where am I? What happened to me?" he asked under his breath.

"Your friends, they are safe and, as I told you, you are in the Holy Land of the Holy Screech. Look at this *land in the eye,* er, map. This is my home."

"But where is it?"

"Well, I think what you mean, this is not the place that you call er... earth, ... we are not on earth..."

"Where are we?" Half-Tongue shouted. He was under the effects of his new and unaccountable surroundings, and to complicate his embarrassment, there was this talking owl. The owl was not at all how he was supposed to look like. He was tall, an inch at least taller than Half-Tongue, and his face, apart from the beak and feathers, did not feel owlish at all. Neither was it a human face. Larger eyes, but not sitting in round niches. The mouth felt human, but with more distinct elevations around the lines, and those ridges were talking about dangerous teeth.

"As I said," the owl hawked, "We are in the Holy Land of the Holy Screech. I think, in your tongue, you would call this place, hm, magical or a different universe."

"You mean it is enchanted? But how did we come here? There must be some magical door to enter and exit? I do not remember anything. Who or what brought me here?" he said.

"Well," the owl hawked again, "It is a little bit complicated. I will try to explain everything later. I think you would not understand now."

"Oh," Half-Tongue sat down on a small, sofa-looking object by the window.

"Please excuse me, but I am going to be awkward," the owl continued, "I may switch to my tongue when I am home, and sometimes you will find my expressions hard to understand. My language is full of metaphors and metonymies. My mother tongue is not in the same state as yours, we use fewer words to describe things."

"Oh," said Half-Tongue, again; the lengthy explanation diverted his attention from his confusion and fear.

"But forgive me, I need to see my *youngs*, they must be awakening right now," said the owl, pulverizing to dusk in the window.

Half-Tongue looked around. The room was at least 10-15 meters high, but awfully narrow on the inside. The walls were filled with books, scrolls, and clay tablets. The books were laid on the shelves with their face towards the room, not the way he was used to, the thin spine towards the reader. The room looked like the internal skeleton of a giant whale from the inside, because the builders furnished the room all around the walls with vast rings and curves for the books. The reader could fascinate themselves by the intriguing and curious covers, which were abundant in colors and animal figures. Only one book differed from the coloured mass, a big gray book. Half-Tongue drew closer because the gray looked strangely changing from where he was standing. The cover was furry and the breeze from the window slightly altered the shades of the book every time it ruffled the hairs.

There was only one door in the tower and one window right next to it. A cuckoo clock stood opposite the door. Half-Tongue noticed a painting above the cuckoo clock. An old, gray owl was sitting in front of a book, the beak coloured in black ink, head and eyes turned away from the pages. He looked out of the window because the old gray was looking in that direction. The sun was striking the water as the surface of the sea was bouncing up and down.

He was examining the cuckoo clock when Arethusa returned.

"So strange. This clock," started Half-Tongue in deep inquisitive tones.

"This cuckoo clock was planned and built by a druid a thousand years ago," he hawked, "Mind you, the second hand has stuck on the hour hand, and this slows the whole machine down."

"I do not mind the minutes, this must be slow, though. I mean the hours."

"In the morning and evening when the sun goes up or down, I mean when it is close to the surface, I think almost to eleven and from four o'clock, when the sun is close to the surface, the waves will bounce up and down to strike the number of the hours. You will not have to rely on the position of the sun. So even if the tide is low or high, you will know the hour. We have very different sea movements here. I mean from what you can know. In England. You must be patient," he sighed, adding, "You must be patient with everything around here... It is true that this land belongs to my kind, but obviously, we have our... so-called... er... enemies, who turn things upside down. Now, we often turn to otherworldly creatures for help, and not everything works as expected. Sometimes these things just hang here, like that sea magic, and nobody uses them. Sometimes they turn our land into a mess. I should not forget to mention that we often needed help to defend our land and we are very grateful for any help."

He silenced for a minute to let Half-Tongue digest what he said.

"This sea magic was implemented by him, the druid, too. We care only for dawn and dusk. The druid is... akin to you...," he sighed, releasing a light pitch tone as the air was leaving his beak, "An overlord..."

"An overlord? For what? For whom?"

"His story is the most interesting one, my dear friend. He was an exile in my world, a Seeker of Light, he was."

"Looking for consciousness, religious or what?"

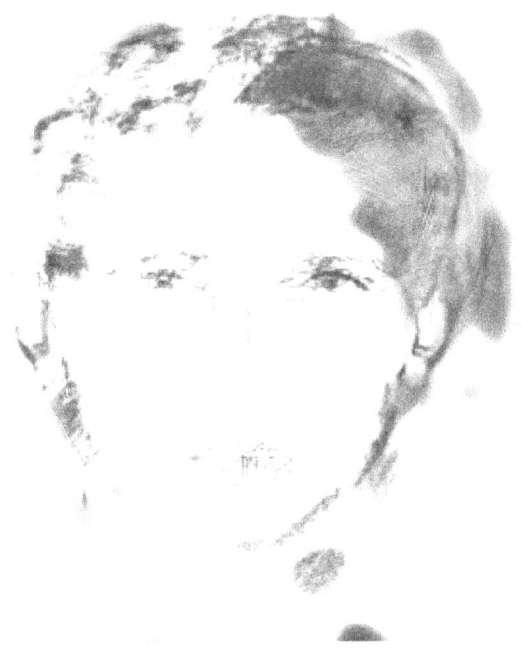

"Well, druid, his story is rather a story of physics. He led his people to battle against a great powerful army. They were surrounded and no help came. He was fighting with such fierce power, his force concentrated in his punches and slashes, that his powerful internal particles were leaving his body. His greatest enemy, an unruly overlord, was destroyed by his hands with such force of emotions and physical power, that he lost most of his body mass. He has been looking for that light ever since."

"You mean his body was made of light?"

"Some."

"He must be a special creature," Half-Tongue slanted his head to his side, "not human."

"Yes, he is more powerful than you, or even me. His ways are hard to understand, he exiled in our land. Let's just see..., would you be so kind as to fetch a book for me from behind that door? It is a gray book, with the head of an owl on the cover, you will see it immediately. It is on the left."

Half-Tongue tried to open the door.

"Oh, I forgot to tell you how to open. It is so obvious for me. There is a knocking spell on it. Ta-ta-ta, pause, ta-ta-ta-ta, ta-ta, ta, ta," knocked Arethusa on the door. The door opened up, creaking back the same rhythm.

"I do not think this is really ... a safe one."

"What do you mean?"

"Anybody can overhear it."

"Nobody can come here. This knocking spell was an exercise for the children."

The owl opened the gray book which Half-Tongue fetched from the next room.

"Hmmm..." he grumbled, "I think the overlord left this chapter unfinished. I'll try to explain."

He pointed at the lower surface of the cuckoo clock.

"Before the season of spring, that small spring will rise to that letter of the inscription, the W, and in autumn it falls back to where it sits now. I don't exactly remember the mechanics he conjured for the winter and summer. I think they were not on the clock. I've forgotten, excuse this to me," he turned away from Half-Tongue to mumble, "It must have been on the compass, or the watch..."

"But I can see four letters on the clock's face," said Half-Tongue.

"Yes, they are the letters of the word *Wind*. The overlord created this clock to stand through time. It helped him to find his ways... in this land and time. The Wind lords were named after their deeds later."

"*Wind lords*? Are they here? Can I talk to them?"

"They left our world after the battle of Mordant Go Uh. The dragons of the neighborhood land attacked us, for it was in their king's want to rule this land. We do not have *kings* whatsoever," he added, "The dragons, as you know, are vast and very heavy animals due to their acidic blood and fluids. The Wind lords lulled all the winds of our lands so that the dragons could not fly long distances. Most of them died."

"But if the wind doesn't blow, how can the sea move?" asked Half-Tongue thinking.

"I told you, it is magic," sighed Arethusa, "The winds have a different story."

"Oh, I've forgotten," Half-Tongue said apologetically.

"Do not worry, Half-Tongue, I must be patient," Arethusa heartened him up, sighing, "It is rather hard to fly without the wind."

"Is it not impossible?"

"Not for us, not for us," he answered, "There are not many things impossible for us, you know. But dragons... dragons are the... oh, I'm forgetting, I want to tell you about this later."

"I think you can explain it now, I..."

Arethusa interrupted.

"First you must meet The Owl Dirndl."

"The owl Drin... An owl?"

"Well, yes, he was born an owl. His life is a little bit different now, I mean from that of an owl... His duty is to sow the winds in the heart of our land, where the administrative bodies sit," said he, leering at Half-Tongue, "It works, thank heaven! Owls do not have to worry about flying in the capital, Half-Tongue."

"You have strange names, is it what you call me, Half-Tongue? And what does his name mean, that Drindel?"

"The Owl Dirndl. It is not his true name, rather his title or status. We are all given unique names when we are freshly born, but that changes when we *become something else* in ... our society. His name roughly means *he who was responsible for the air movement in the administrative district after the Wind War.* Before the war he was responsible for the administration of nuances and matters related to otherworldly creatures," Arethusa added, "He was called *he who was responsible for the nuances and matters related to otherworldly creatures during the Wind War.*"

"Why is his name in past tense? He *is* responsible for the winds now, is he not?"

"Ah, that's a matter of historicity and administration. When we name someone, we give a name that would be meaningful from the future. Anytime. Therefore, we name everyone as if we saw them from the future. From a book. So, we always must use long names. It is not his full name though, as... you see... and he will not always be The Owl Dirndl," he said, "But I will return to this later," he added hastily.

"Oh. You said I must see him? But where is the capital? And I do not really understand why you have Greek names."

"You can find some books written by humans of your world in the attic. We follow a tradition, having Greek names, or roman, when talking to humans. It was easier for the lords.

"Oh, are they human?"

"Like your once and future king. And his wizard."

Half-Tongue looked at him surprised.

"Hm? Once and future king? It's King Arthur, isn't he? Was he here? And is he here?" Half-Tongue got confused.

"Merlyn... or his owl? I was his owl," he smiled at Half-Tongue with a telling smile.

"I want to know how I can go home. You said this is not a magic land..."

"I would like you to come with me to the capital. I'd need to flick you."

"Flick me?" Half-Tongue asked in a half angry, half surprised tone.

"You'll see," the owl hawked into his ears, "But first you need to leave the tower. The energy may destroy my books. I'll explain how you can leave. The door is behind the clock," he picked up a book from the table and put his beak on a picture.

"C-lock," he pointed at a rectangle, "It opens up for a special trigger," Arethusa stepped closer to the C-lock, and put his beak on the minute hand first and then on the hour hand- to turn it toward the sun in the window. Now the C-lock said ten to ten.

"The two hands will heat up in a second to activate a trigger to open the door."

"So, I go through?" asked Half-Tongue who became anxious because he heard strange noises as the door creaked to open up.

"Yes. After you enter, you must go down to the end of the stairs. You will see a door. It is a special door. There is a mirror opposite. That door is a magical two-way door. It can lead outside of the tower or to the corridor that runs to the library under the tower."

"Underground?"

"Yes. There are an immense number of books there, and it's airtight. The door protects the library as well," the owl stretched his head, "Do you know that legend about Archimedes and how he managed to burn up Roman ships to defend his land?"

"No."

"According to legend, Archimedes built a vast mirror to concentrate the rays of the sun," he silenced. Half-Tongue did not fully understand what he wanted to say.

"And?"

"Well, the mirror was directed towards the ships to burn them. So this mirror, down there, is there to defend us from intruders and also to open the door. In direct sunlight, the mirror will burn a dragon alive," he turned his head towards Half-Tongue to be lit up in the light of the sun. "Light and dark, energy and power, they all work differently in my world," he sighed, "I'll explain a little what you will also hear from the Owl Dirndl. In the capital where we go."

"So... how does the door open?"

"As I said it is a two way- door. Out or down...."

"Then it must be some magic? Double entrance?" Half-tongue became curious.

"Well, this part," the owl hawked, "Not that... way. The door is built halfway in the ground."

"Halfway?"

"The lower part of the door leads to the chamber down and the upper part out."

"I will also have to climb then," said Half-Tongue laughing.

"Yes, only the upper part of the door will open for you. The lower part is sealed."

"I still don't know what I'll have to do to open the door."

"Keep the torch I give you close to the mirror. The light of the flames will trigger the magic. When the door opens you will have to be very fast."

Half-tongue looked at Arethusa with his eyebrows drawn.

"Why do I have to move fast?"

"Otherwise, you burn yourself or get stuck in the door. The sun is very low now so we can start out. You can't keep the door open with the torch. You will need it in the dark. Daylight would destroy you. We do not burn anything for long down there, the smoke could sweep in when we open the underdoor."

"Underdoor," repeated Half-Tongue.

"The door to the library. The lower part of the door."

"Ah."

The upper part of the door blurred into the color of the light from the torchlight; a red glowing mist, reflected in the mirror. Half-Tongue elbowed himself up to ground level and swiftly sneaked through the opening. He lifted the torch from the ground. The moment he turned it up the door started to return to its original material, the structure of the birch planks appeared again, now from the outside.

"Fast. Too fast," he murmured, "I would not want to become part of it."

He crawled into a safe position in the benevolent shaft of his torch. He found niches in the rock to stabilize his feet and a round rock to sit on. He could look around now- it was nothing like what he could see from the window. The holy land was dressed in strange colors, shady hues of purple and yellow.

"Might have some coating on that window," he muttered to himself again. He was struck by these colors, the purple of the sky forming geometrical shapes of squares, hexagons and octagons, and the rock under his feet, in the shades of slightly lit yellow. It had a certain flare of a mystic shining he could not define.

He waited for his eyes to get used to this new color scheme and its effect on his mind. He started to climb down the rock surface. It felt somewhat sticky, which made his climb easier. He spotted the owl under, in the bottom of the valley. He started to descend towards his direction.

"So which way, oh you said, you would flick me."

"Yes, and as I said you will experience a certain "flare," he pronounced this last word rattling his throat, "The flicking may ruin my books, it needs its space."

"So does it hurt?"

"I can assure you that you will not feel any pain."

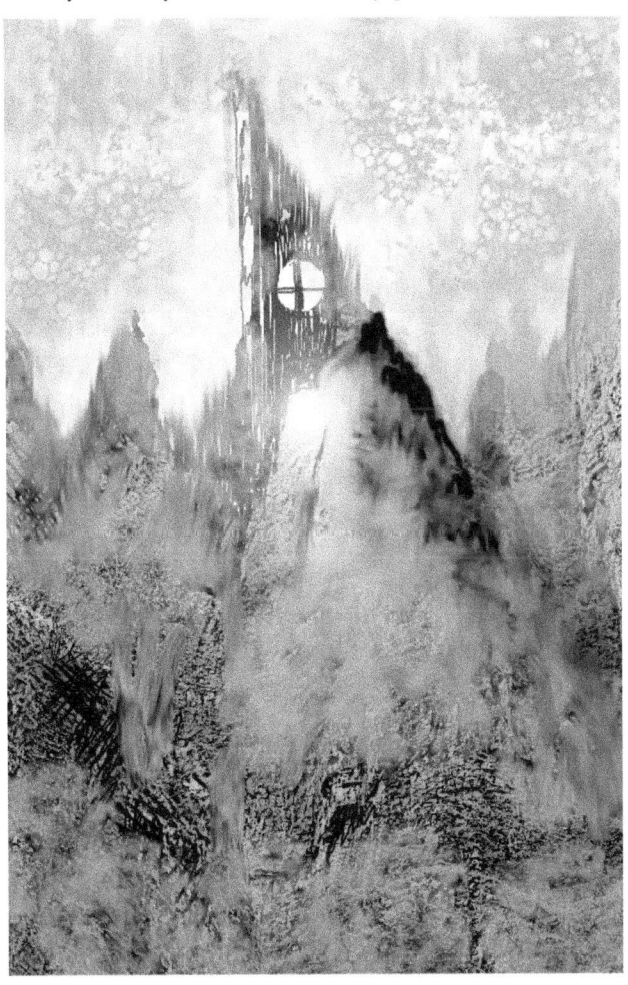

Part 5

Chronicles of a capital

"Hoooooooowwwwllllllll......" Half -Tongue was screaming his lungs to the Owl when he landed on stable ground at last. "AAAHHHHHHH..." he was still shouting when Arethusa poked him.

"You are safe, Half-Tongue, stop yelling."

"BUT I AM LOOOOOSSSIIING MY BALAAAANCE..." continued Half-Tongue, who was extremely overwhelmed by the effects of the journey.

"So where are we?" he asked after he could calm down.

"Look out, Half-Tongue. This is the capital of my holy land," Arethusa croaked.

"Wow", said Half-Tongue, having been surprised by the sudden change to the scenery of the capital.

"This is stunning! This is nothing I have ever seen before! A town of towers! These towers, they are awesome, they are beautiful!"

"Some of it was built by my ancestors. And some by their descendants. And some by us."

"Why, they look like lacework! Why, are those, what are those? Very intricate, indeed!"

"Well, Half- Tongue, the structure of these towers is given by their very building material."

"Which is?"

"Dragons." Arethusa said under his dark eyebrows.

"Dragons? Hell..." Half-Tongue felt a little gloom around his stomach. "What the hel..." he muttered half-faced as he hit something with his foot trying to step closer to have a better look at the structures.

"The board..." Arethusa hawked with surprise, "You stepped on the board, my dear."

"What board?"

"This is the board emblem for this viewpoint. The Ancestors' view."

"It is nice," he said, looking into the distance.

"Let's go now, it is getting too dark, we will see nothing."

"How strange, this dusk still gives you this very good view."

"Not after total darkness. We do not have moons. There will not be anything to reflect for the rocks. Let's go now," Arethusa said, his legs finding the way down to the capital city.

"I am following," Half-Tongue answered softly, out of tiredness.

They were climbing and jumping their way down to the valley that spread in front of them in its purplish yellowish, almost sparkling colors. The towers came closer and closer, to illustrate what Arethusa said earlier. The sharpness of dragon teeth shone from the top of the buildings.

"This is awesome and... disgusting... and," he said when they arrived at the legs of the closest tower, "Dragon teeth, you say?" he turned to Arethusa for the answer, "How fearful!"

"Yes, they are fearful," Arethusa said.

"But they are so close to each other!"

"These towers do not serve the same purpose as in your world."

"You mean to look out?"

"Well, yes. This constellation is born from our ways and stands in life, our very ways of existence."

Half-Tongue started to understand Arethusa's speech, which sometimes was awkward. It felt decipherable now.

"So, what do these towers do?"

"Did you look back at the tower before I flicked you? In the valley, when you were climbing down?"

"I had no idea, but is it the same... "design?" He added the word with some careful sarcasm.

"Design. Yes. One way to put it." Arethusa smothered a smile between his beaks, "The structure is built on a dragon skeleton, whilst the building holds a vast number of books. And the top... it is like a scalp," he added.

"The teeth?"

"The teeth. They look like the open mouth of a dragon from above. Not only a scalp, but to scare off."

"So, all these towers serve the same purpose?" whispered Half-Tongue.

"Yes, the same structures. All of them are rib cages."

"Of dragons?"

"Most. And some other creatures and models of our ancestors. Before the war we did not have this exquisite corpse collection," he sighed.

Half-Tongue felt a little estranged.

"So many and so close... other creatures?"

"Some. I will tell you everything in the libraries. It is going to be much easier for me to show this, all my world to you... in them."

"Still some look like lighthouses!?"

"Those styles! The owners...," he sighed, "Well, I could even call them a political faction, I mean based on all that screeching and hawking and hooting we went through..."

"They had their own ideas, you mean?"

"Well, yes. They thought that the lighthouse design, well, added some fearfulness to the way the city looked. And one way, they were right. But let's move."

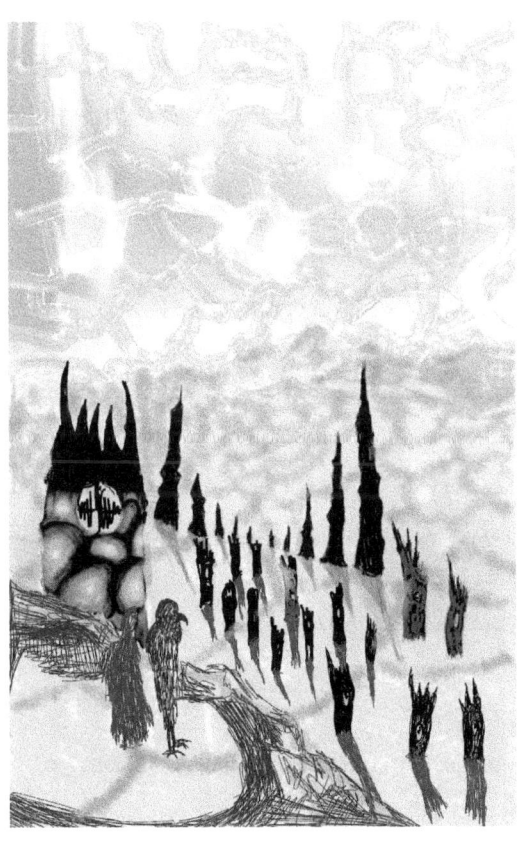

They were standing in front of a longish, barrel shaped black tower.

"This, Half-Tongue, is the Black library. The most ancient, curious and venerable building of our time," he said, slightly clattering with his beaks," and maybe all times... We are not going to enter. The turbine tower is at work until the light holds."

"Turbine tower?" Half-Tongue did not understand how these things were connected.

"Follow me, I shall introduce you to the owl Dirndl. He is... well, he works in the turbine tower, and we will need to relieve him to talk to him."

"What do you use the turbine tower for?"

"Do you feel the breeze on your skin?"

"It is stronger than before. Oh, you said the other Owl is responsible for the winds, you only have winds in the capital then? And that low breeze everywhere else?"

"Well, around the islands, yes. We flew more before the war. Now all the winds are lulled, and we can control who can fly in our lands as you know. 2000 tonnes are almost impossible to hold in the air without the winds."

"Well, not jets."

"You mean aircrafts?" the Owl looked at him with curious understanding." They do not exist in my world. The day may come when they will, but the technological advancements in my world work differently than in yours."

"Now, you say it, you don't need them, really."

"Aircrafts, not. What I meant is that this world is so strongly based on pure energy that we don't need it."

"Still, you need help."

"Well, and I oftentimes have to say this. *We are abundant in power, but we cannot always use it*," he hawked, "We needed the Wind lords to create ideas. We also need all the books, so we can use it," he roughly hawked again.

"Yes. All that magic you were talking about. Do they all come from the Wind lords?"

"Oh, no. We can use those books to create them. But let us go on to the turbine."

"I don't want you to be too surprised. Well, first of all, this tower, the turbine tower, is my major dwelling place."

"You mean your house?"

"Yes, as you say. You will meet the Owl Dirndl in this tower which houses the source of the winds. The Owl Dirndl will show you his face in a certain lamp room. I hope I prepared you well," he sighed through his beaks, "Just imagine, there is a working turbine in this house," and he looked at Half-Tongue hopefully.

"Well, I don't know what novelties you have for me..., but I feel like I am getting used to this."

"All right then. Let's enter," he pressed his beak into the middle of the door.

"What are you doing?"

"That's the keyhole."

"And your beak is the key?"

"Yes, exactly as you say it."

"Look at this!" They came up to a skeletal structure glooming from the dark.

"What is this?"

"This is not life size. A spider - miniaturized."

"And that?" Half-Tongue pointed at a larger structure coming to light as they were heading ahead, "How strange! But truly very similar to what I have seen in the tower!"

"That was, what you saw, was the full ribcage of a dragon. This... is one of my ancestors."

"Your ancestors... they were vast."

"Evolution and genetic jumps, they are different in my world. The more strenuous an environment is, the likelier the changes are, as you may know. Some of us can shift their size, even now."

"You mean become bigger, even bigger than... this?"

"This is not big, my dear," the owl said with a certain darkness in his voice, "I can become smaller too," he added.

"Why... you have so many books here, strange books, and THIS.... This takes the cake..." and he showed him the book with the same furry cover that captured his curiosity in the tower.

"We had quite the collection before, but the Wind lords, recreated the palimpsest, because it had been destroyed by the dragons during the wind wars..., but after that, the Wind lords used a special formula, called

Stomachion combinatorics, and since then all written word, ever written in any world appears in mine."

"WOW..." said Half-Tongue, "You cannot have everything in your library..."

"Obviously not... This is my favorite collection. And I have the books I work with... When I flick into other worlds, I use these to familiarize myself with the other world."

"Travel books?"

"Sort of..., often a travel book has no mindset of a single author to show a world. But I want to show you something... it is in the lamp; I mean the written words of the **worlds.**"

Arethusa raised his wings and sprung himself into the corridor they came through. He landed in front of a wooden door which still bore the raw surface of a birch tree.

"Look through the keyhole... can you see anything?"

"I can see lightning..., really strange, a sphere..., there are flashes..., this sphere is really strange..."

"Have you ever seen a plasma lamp at home, Half-Tongue?"

"No, not really, is it how it looks like, what is this?"

"It IS The Owl Dirndl. Let me switch him off."

"Is this The Owl? What do you mean?"

"Now switching him off... from this... state is something like when you switch off a plasma lamp. Do you know how a plasma lamp works? But first let me see him," Arethusa looked through the keyhole, then scratched his head.

"Hm...", he grumbled, "He seems to be in a... We cannot go to the room now; all the air would escape for good. It is quite hard to produce these gasses, you know..."

"What gasses?"

"The gasses in the room. The room is sealed, you would say, hera... herma... hermatis...", Arethusa didn't seem to find the word.

"Hermetically?" asked Half-Tongue.

"Yes, I think, so there is a hermetic seal... to hold the air in the room."

"WHAT IS HAPPENING IN THERE?" cried Half-Tongue out because the air was being filled up from the room with louder and harsher humming and crackling.

"This is the Owl Dirndl and the lamp. I mean he is... the lamp...," pulling Half-Tongue out of the corridor.

"This is a lamp the Wind lords came up with to solve the word stream of consciousness flowing in."

"What?"

"So, this lamp and the Owl Dirndl are there to curb the stream of words... In the beginning we had a slow, but steady flow of different publication formats. The weirdest one for me is that one on top in the library. It's a talking point. I'll show you."

The owl crawled back to the library. He raised his left wing to a dark point in the corner close to him.

"I can't see anything."

"I've got better eyes than you. Take this magnifier."

"Well, it is a point, but why talking? I don't hear anything."

"I can hear it."

"What does it say?"

"Well, translated... Let me listen to it... *So now, mow, row, well ain't you hear it bro... What's the point in talking,*", he paused, "I had been listening to it for a while and it usually reverts back to this one sentence... what's the point in talking... Gibberish for me, but probably has every meaning somewhere else..."

"Not that gibberish. Like poetry. Feels like a metaphor for defiance. A talking point that is talking about the meaninglessness of talking. I mean this whole thing. You know I am a poet."

"Well, yes."

"But you said it is the written word. In a point."

"Yeah. Basically, the text is written. In the point. But it also talks."

"How could it be a point then?" asked Half-Tongue.

"This one, yes. We only *see* it as a point. I can't read it, anyway."

"How do you know then that there is a text?"

"I flicked to the other side."

"Of the point?"

"Yes."

"What was there then?"

"Well, not a point. Something on the other side turned up on this side as a talking point. That's what I can see. That poem or whatever. We have these anomalies around the words. That is why the lords had to invent the lamp. To curb what the words were doing."

"How strange this whole thing is... This lamp and words, as if it was just a stupid pun."

"Well, yes. Every word is a *dead* metaphor. My world is a metaphor," Arethusa fell into the curious mindset of a gloomy explanation, "You can continue... everything is a metaphor for something else."

"We could work this back into... anything I say is dead," said Half-Tongue laughing."

"No, no," said Arethusa, "This just means that everything that you say is a metaphor."

"You said the word *dead*."

"It is just the metaphor."

"Oh. I'll probably need a lot of time to understand your world."

"Here is this book for you, Stomachion within," said Arethusa, blinking at Half-Tongue.

He took the book from his wings. He has never seen anything like this before; the cover felt crude and soft at the same time, he would not be able to tell how.

List of magic numbered and named. Described - said the cover.

"What is the feeling, what kind of material is this?"

"Jellyfish. The skin of jellyfish."

Half-Tongue turned the page.

"First page," he read it out, "How strange."

"You will have the page number on odd pages to precede every even page with text."

"Strange. Why?"

"This is a mythical book, Half-Tongue."

"I think it would be best if you told me about it and then I would just then find a word for it. I don't understand. Do you have myths in these or is it old? Like existing since mythical times?"

"Both of these are not true. I might have used the wrong word. A word that better describes my feelings than the facts. This book lists magic. I mean the steps of enacting magic."

"Oh. You mean it describes magic. I think I am starting to understand you."

"It was written before we were able to curb the words in that lamp. Well, around the same time. The Wind lords wrote books with the help of the lamp. These things meant a lot of problems at that time."

"Second page," Half-Tongue paged on.

"Turn over, it is on the even side."

"Come to think of it, the text will only appear on the left side. Numbering starts where you start it," he laughed out "So is this about the left side?"

"No, it is about the numbering. It adjusts to the very physical nature of the book. This one, for example," he paged back to the first page in the book, "is the first page in every book. Anything you do, this will always be the first page."

"Now you say it, the physical numbers will not correspond to anything after that, I mean not accordingly. The second page will be your third page and so on."

"What is a page, Half-Tongue?"

"Well, where I come from, it is one side of the paper."

"And on a parchment or a scroll?"

"They were not numbered."

"They could be. When did you last open a scroll?"

"I think I would know where I am in the text."

"Would you? How?"

"I mean texts came with figures and..." he said after a little silence, "AAAAHH... you mean this was a scroll before."

"That is your story. Look at the first page. I mean on the other side. What does it say?"

Half-Tongue read out a table of contents from the page.

Half-Tongue was studying the drawings on the page.

"So, what is this all about?"

"The very essence of what they do. The stomachion combinatorics. Turn to that page."

"All of this," he said, "seems to be very interesting. The pictures are even more interesting. But I still don't understand. Stomachion? Is that a Greek word?"

"Archimedes' stomachion was something you may know about."

"No idea."

"Well, it is a dissection puzzle. It is like all the mathematical problems in those times, Euclid, Archimedes, Pythagoras..., they all tried to solve geometrical problems with the help from these puzzles."

"What does it have to do with magic?" Half-Tongue asked with fading enthusiasm in his voice.

"Well, in a nutshell, all problems are like that. They are all puzzles. Even magic. You will be more understanding later, when you have seen more of my world."

Half-Tongue nodded agreeably.

"I think you would be more interested in reading about our history. This book," he turned to a large sized one on the curves, "is the translation of the palimpsest. The Wind lords translated. Originally there existed The Holy Chronicle of The Holy Land," the owl sighed, "and this is its translation, to a human tongue."

"When the dragons took hold of this tower, they scratched out the letters," Arethusa continued, "but left their marks and dragon blood on the parchment. After the war the original text was recovered, but the scratching by the dragons could not be totally undone."

"It looks strange. The surface. As if moving, but how? I could not put my finger on it."

"It's like a hologram in your world..."

"So, what is happening on the surface?"

"It is the bosons."

"How?"

"The bosons don't decay fast. The particles of my universe, you can see the difference in the structure, but obviously the energy fields are different, and it is the energy that changes it..., I think the best way to put it is that these bosons are more active because there is more energy... all the bosons relate differently to each other, of course. this special effect would not be present on the cover of the palimpsest books in your world. The many ancient texts which only survived on palimpsests in your world, are like this text, but the physics is different. And this changes everything... gives us something you do not have."

"Like magic."

"Yes and no. If I spoke my mind, I would not call it magic. Magic in your world means things you do not understand. And I do understand my world. I do also understand your world, druid."

"But? I don't understand why the other books don't do this, they are the same bosons aren't they," Half-Tongue was arguing, losing his patience to frustration.

"You still do not understand. They are the same bosons but the way they are layered are different. Because of the changes."

"Aaaahhh, you mean that it was destroyed, and then put together again, uhuh." Half-Tongue smiled a little.

"Yes, that. And then again, look at this one," he pulled off another furry looking book from the curves, "this book was created from the skin of the space spider."

"Space spider?" Half-Tongue said, his eyebrows pulled to despair.

"This world... builds up like a spiderweb, the time and space spiders, the two spiders that work out our worlds. As they pull the next line around the other, our worlds are created on top of the old worlds as a new layer but building from the old layer as well. So, you see my world existed before yours, yours was built on my layer. It is different on a subatomic level... It was made on different levels of energy."

"I wonder what's in the core?" asked Half-Tongue.

"I knew you would ask," hooted the owl, "Those radials that help to build the web meet in the middle of all these worlds, but we could never find out about that thing in the middle, I mean... This web is all connected on some deep level we don't understand. Like the dark energy and matter in your world."

"I do not understand."

"Imagine the universe as a spiderweb. Where the circular strings are timelines building and growing from each other and then the linear lines are spatial manifestations of energy, matter and I mean space itself, you get that?"

"Yes."

"I would add up to a totally black picture at the end, of course because the number of lines is unlimited, but in structure you could eventually discover a spiderweb."

"OK."

"These lines are so dense, they intertwine. And any movement in the structure will cause changes somewhere else at a certain energy level, and this changes things. Well, you change things, but you are changed as well. The Wind lords can feel these indentations and move within the spiderweb."

"What is this about these changes? It would mean that what I do or what happens to me is not based on my being, but the whole spiderweb."

"Na, that is not that simple. This whole structure is, well imagine it is just too big to work like that. When something changes here, it means tiny changes for you. The 1/100000000000000000000000000000000000 weight of one of your bosons may be lost for you."

"Oh OK, but am I not affected by the whole web? So, everything changes in me every time and this whole web is unlimited so where does this go... it blows your mind..."

"Well, nobody understands," Arethusa was hawking, "This is something of an axiom in my culture. There are things we will never see."

"I have always hated to think about these things eventually," said Half-Tongue, "The fact that you can never understand and explain everything ultimately and can just accept that yours is only a point of view... This will always be haunting."

"Hmm." the owl said, "Understandable."

Arethusa crawled up to a curve on the left and said, "Let me show you something."

"It is all runes and criss-cross to me."

"I'll have to translate," and the owl read the text out from the book.

> The island system of the holy land is 60000.78, in recurring decimal miles long, and 2120.34 miles in recurring decimal broad. By the farthest isles. By the line of the Southeast, which is the SE line exactly, as it goes through the ranges of Mordant Go Uh, the land is 84800 miles long.

"How can this be? Your map," Half-Tongue pointed at a picture in the book, "it looks distorted... by these lines at least, really," he took a pencil from his pocket, "Look at this. I can draw a square, like this," and he drew a picture of a right-angled triangle to show the owl why it would not add up.

"Ah, Pythagoras. Yet, it is that length. In this *land in the eye...* a map. They hid the land in this distortion."

Half-Tongue's eyebrows pulled closer to his hairline. Something was not right, but he decided to ignore the numbers for now.

"From the dragons?"

"Not just them," Arethusa set his eyes on Half-Tongue, "When the dragons came they read the palimpsest and did not find us. Maps are important for newcomers. When they came, they could not see where we were. They could not fly over the land to survey either, because they were too heavy."

"It would be an enormous distance up, I mean if these numbers are right somehow..., this land is vast. The view would always be distorted."

"Yes," and he read on, "And there are in the land three races, owls, dragons and lice."

"No spiders?"

"There are no spiders," Arethusa looked at Half-Tongue.

"Why are there no spiders in your palimpsest. It says three races inhabited this land and one of them was lice. Where are the spiders?"

"This palimpsest was written by my ancestors... about the coming of the lice... as yours about the coming of Vikings... they did not see the spiders in this land. They are vast creatures, they shed their skin all around the worlds, but they do not belong in this world," he dug his head into the book again to read,

> *The first inhabitants were the owls who came through the earth and first owled this Holy Land, as is, fully. Then happened it, that the dragons came through the air, from the air with long wings, not many came, and landed first in the northern part of Hydra.*

"Your history resembles ours. Very strong parallels, indeed."

"Do you think so?" Arethusa smiled slanting his beak to the left, "Let me ask you something."

"Go ahead."

The owl pulled up to a curve to lift off another book. He opened it up in the middle and put it on a table.

"What do you make of these?"

The owl Arethusa and Half-Tongue were leaning above the book. Half-Tongue became intrigued by the strange drawings he saw.

"What are these?" he asked.

"Well, my friend, that is exactly my question to you. What do you think these drawings depict?"

"Hmmm," Half-Tongue was hesitant, but interested, "Hmmm, I could think of one or two things..."

"What do you mean? Not one?"

"Well, it's really a stitchwork here," he said.

"HMMM" said the owl, "You have not read the story. Let me read it to you. I need to translate it to you anyway."

"Yeah, I noticed you have some quite interesting symbols around here. Is it your alphabet?"

"Well, not anymore. It is the ancient language of my forefathers. Let me read and translate,

> It all happened at the very noon of darkness. An undarkened moment. The love of those. It all went against the universe.

"This part is a love poem," said the owl.

"So, I hear, by whom?"

"From whom to whom?"

"Well, yes, but also, who wrote it down?"

"Ah, that. We don't know. The poem tells the love of the small dragon."

"To whom?"

"To the lady Owl."

"What? You mean this is a love story between a dragon and an owl?"

"Well, yes," the owl cleared his throat noisily, "Let me read."

> *"Father, I was standing on a hill*
> *And one drop of water fell on my lip.*
> *When it later started to rain..."*

"How beautiful! From a dragon! And how strange!"

> *"It was like when you are thirsty*
> *The rain coming down*
> *And that one drop is your answer."*

"You are really good at reading poetry," said Half-Tongue.

"You are a poet. Do you understand?"

Half-Tongue chuckled at the owl's question.

"How, don't you?"

"This text is apocryphal for us. Even cryptic."

"What? The text?

"We store this in stories sections. We only have two and the other one is in the black library."

"I presume..." Half-Tongue was thinking, "So according to legend..., This is a dragon talking to an Owl lady, I understand?"

"Well, yes and then turns to his father."

"Yes, that is obvious, he addresses him. Father," Half-Tongue chuckled again," So, yes, I would say,"

"Well, you should not forget, he was a dragon, he never drank water."

"Ok, I see. So, he is talking to the father to explain his new feelings..."

"Yes?"

"It is not something his father would be open to understand, so I presume he hides his feelings behind this metaphor or metonymy. But how come that you, who always use metaphors and metonymies, do not understand?"

"You can interpret my mind through these metaphors, or metonymies, like the map, the land in the eye. I think simpler than you. Do you understand?"

"Well, yes. It is like a kenning for you."

"A kenning?"

"My ancestors used this same thing in poetry. Like a whale-road."

"Which is the sea? That is simple. I understand those things. But when it comes to complex systematic poetry, we fail."

"Oh, ok. So, who is the father?

"Hmm," hawked Arethusa shaking his head, "Well, this was an open question to the interpreters before you, well, we think... and here I need to tell you that my ancestors knew much more than I do, so, my ancestors thought that the father was an ancient dragon *king*."

"Who attacked you?"

"Well, yes, it may be the same kingdom."

"So, the *small* dragon," he pronounced *small* with a certain hesitation, "thinks he needs this one drop, but it is not the rain, I mean that one drop is not the rain. It is his teardrop,"

"So, what did he mean?"

"He needs those feelings?"

"Oh," said Arethusa smiling, "that."

"Well, did you?"

"Well, he was quite a draconic one, as I read of him in our stories. The small dragon must have been... banished from the family."

"So, what happened to the small dragon and the owl lady?"

"We don't know."

Half-Tongue balanced himself on the nearby table and yawned.

"Well, my friend, you need to sleep."

Part 6

The second coming of the Wind lords

The air was growing thin and light. Five white spots appeared in the distance, the silhouettes of five white men burning into the spotted fabric facade of a black mountain range. The men were anxious. The hot air of the purplish sky was melting in the light of a white sun.

Kurtz bent forward. He could not stand his coat sagging around his knees.

"It is hot," he said.

"Yey," the other men answered.

"I will raise the wind."

They all nodded.

Kurtz swung his arms. Swinging like pendulums, the coat's wings started flapping around his knees after his arms. The wind grew.

"The mouse," he said, "We seem to be at the right time at the right place.

"But that thing... that should not be here." Four said.

"What is it? It is not so close..." Thee looked the way he pointed at, "It is out of our range. I do not know. So why are we here? And... here again," Thee asked plaintively.

Kurtz did not answer, he scratched his forehead impatiently. Thee looked at him asking, "A bird I guess."

"I expect it is dead," said Kurtz.

"Definitely, dead. So, the cat was here."

"That was alive, I guess, I do not know where it has gone."

"The Schrödinger cat?"

"That cat," said Kurtz laughing. Four laughed with him.

"So now what?"

"We find 'im."

"The kid? With no tongue? Here? Why would he be here?"

said Thee.

"Is this his distinctive characteristic? He's got no tongue?"

asked Four whining, "How do we find him?"

"I do not think it is gonna be a problem... here..."

"Oh here... yeah, I have to remind myself **where** we are... where are we?

And how do you know that he is here?"

"Look...," started Kurtz, I do not think it's gonna be a problem..."

"Yeah here, no problems," said Four groaning.

"Four, what's the matter?"

Four groaned.

"So, we are caught somewhere in time and space... again..., here..."

"It is eerily empty. Like Vertical. Do they have the same issues, I wonder?" Four looked at Kurtz asking. They arrived the morning after Half-Tongue and the owl entered the capital of the holy land.

"I do not know anything about what is happening here... the best idea is to go to the house of the Owl Dirndl and see," Kurtz answered.

"Hell, the Owl Dirndl," Mof muttered, "When we were here last time, he was in that lamp."

"Let us see. He is the only contact I can think of now. The owl, I mean Arethusa," and he shook his head, "lives among those rocks. It would be a mess to travel there today."

The others looked at him sighing with relief. Kurtz had always been a comforting and calming presence, always knowing what they should do, always ready with answers to their questions.

"I am forgetting how we have missed you," Thee thanked him with a tired smile.

"Which way are you going to get to the house?" Kurtz said.

"Are you not coming with us?"

"I will join you in an hour at his house, don't worry. I'll... have to look into something... in that library," he pointed in the other direction, toward a tall, dark building.

"Ah, that one... the curiosity shop," Four was smirking at Kurtz, "Please don't be late. And of course, we don't want to go with you. To the black library... no."

"Well," Fife interrupted, "I would like to go with him.... of course, if you don't mind, Kurtz," his baffled eyes stared at him, almost begging for a yes, "I am sure they will find their way in."

"Well, yes," Kurtz murmured under his breath, "I have an idea why he is here... I want to see some old books for the solution."

"The good old Kurtz already knew... I have always loved this in you," Four laughed at him thinking, "All right, just go your ways, we will go ours..." and he started to walk down the road towards the tower in which they thought they would find the meaning for this journey.

Kurtz and Fife turned right towards the direction of the Black Library. They stopped in front of the gate, staring up to the building towering above them. They could not see any owl around the door, no one was answering their knocking either. Kurtz pushed the doors. To his surprise the double birchwood gate gave in without resistance.

"How strange... no magic, no sentinel, what happened to them?" Fife said.

"I don't know... as I said I could not talk to the owl on earth."

"Yes, you have said, why are we here then?"

"I suspect something... when we left, we left something unfinished."

"Unfinished? How? When we stopped all the winds all the dragons died, did they not?"

"I knew something was happening near the border."

"Near the border? Like what?"

"A nest."

"A nest," Fife looked at Kurtz astonished, "Why, you never told us..."

"There was no need. I mean..."

Fife's eyebrows and forehead played out his feelings towards the dumb old CIA reflexes he knew were there in Kurtz.

"No need... I would understand, but not here..."

"All right, I know, it was just too much back then for you."

"So, what nest?" Fife asked edgily.

"Before we left, the border sentinels were reporting certain activity ... in the seas..."

"You don't say that they have the same light under the sea, or what you were talking about a nest?"

"NO, no, no, not the light, not Escence, I mean, but they found dragon eggs on the shores of the island."

"Dragon eggs?"

"They were not hatching though, so we did not take them seriously. They looked dead."

"Then what is the matter? You think there is a nest under the sea you could not find?"

"Yes, I was thinking about this later and things came up from the old books I had read here..."

"What things?"

"About the dragons... that old story about the small dragon and the owl lady."

"The love story?!"

"Yeah, I've been thinking about this for a while, they said something abou..."

"But that story is about the origin of their species!"

Kurtz did not answer. They were talking in the hall of the library, which was the end to many corridors. He was thinking, raising his fingers to Fife to listen.

"We don't have much time... Let me think," and he walked into the corridor on his left.

"Aren't these corridors the same system they use in the towers?"

"Well, yes..."

"Why don't you go to the history section? It is always on the right."

"The book was not in the history section."

"Why not? It was their history."

"It is like apocrypha, they never accepted. It landed in the stories section."

"But you told me...."

"Yeah, I remember what I told you and I even believed that this is true, and I still believe, you just have to look at them."

"Yeah."

"Thing is, they don't accept it."

"That their ancestors are dragons? But even the owl should have seen it... He knows the way they looked before, then what?"

"I think," started Kurtz, but stopped because the door which they were closing in on opened up to frame the dark head of an owl.

"Visitors?" he hawked.

"Yes, sentinel, we are visitors."

"Where from?"

"Do you not recognise us?" asked Fife, who remembered the owl.

"Well, let me just see you from the close... hmmm," he was rattling his wings in awe, "My old friends... the Wind lords!"

"We need a book...." started Fife.

"Let me greet you in the proper manner my friends!"

Kurtz interrupted him to stop a tirade of hawking and wing rattling.

"We are really grateful for your kind idea, my friend, but we are in urgent need."

"Oh, my..." said the owl thinking, "Did you come to help us with the bubble matters? I am ready to assist you in any way I can."

Kurtz and Fife shouted at the same time.

"The bubble matters?"

The owl plugged his ears.

"My, my... How come you don't know? I gathered you already met Arethusa, and you came for the book...."

"What book?"

"The book you wanted. What is it, which one?" He was shaking his head, surprised that they had not met Arethusa.

"Oh, I need that book with the stories, the stories of the small dragon and the owl."

"Oh, that. Why would you need that? Anyway, it is in that corner above the lamp. The blue one. That is the only blue book in this library."

"Well, thank you..." Kurtz picked the book from the shelf system.

"Let me just see...," he plunged his head into the book to search for the part he came for. Fife reluctantly poked his arm and said in a low voice:

"Hey, what is the other book? I can go get it. Is it here as well?"

"You could even find out for yourself," Kurtz muttered, diving into the book again.

"Find out, find out," he murmured half angrily, half surprised, "We most probably need some geography book, the bottom of the sea, but where? I might find some atlas," he continued murmuring to himself while he was going along the corridor back to the hall.

"Fact section, that is in the middle," he took the Fact corridor and entered a huge library room, which was empty and dark.

"My god... how am I gonna see anything in here?"

"Just take my hand," giggled Kurtz, who had finished with the Book of Stories and silently followed Fife to the library.

"Oh yes, the Escence... I totally forgot about it."

Fife touched Kurtz causing their skin glow up in the dark intensely.

"It gives us enough light to find an atlas," said Kurtz.

"That was my idea, the palimpsest."

"The palimpsest does not have the data we need."

"Let's take this one, with the full island system on the cover. It looks like Greece."

"As it should. Everything else is hidden in the palimpsest."

"So, what about the Book of Stories? I mean the story."

"Yes, here," and he pulled up the book from his pocket. It was glowing in the dark in its blue cover.

"How strange," said Fife, "the color changes from blue to green..."

"Probably that's us..."

"The Escence?"

"It looks like it."

"Open it."

Kurtz opened the book and the pages lit up in their light even shinier.

"How shiny!" said Fife.

"Hell yes," Kurtz murmured, "the light energizes the electrons on the... parchment, and they emit photons..."

"Yeah, I know this, but it is even shinier than the cover."

"It is the color of the cover. The blue."

"Why?"

"That's the colors. The cover has some different wavelengths."

"Oh, that... anyway, what was the story, what was in the story you wanted to know?"

"Do you know the full story?"

"Not exactly. I would have found out by now what you wanted."

"Now, yes, the book tells the story of a small dragon, who was excommunicated because of his size and left his kingdom."

"That was clear so far..."

"I'll find that page for you... wait."

As Kurtz was going through the book, the pages illuminated their faces stronger from the reflected light. They looked like two spectres in that dark corner of the Black Library. Kurtz put his finger on the line, he started to read, following the text under.

> There he was with the lady owl for a night, escaping from the dragonfire of his kin. Then they laid their nest by the shore, and under water.

"Oh, that is what you are looking for, but does it give you a physical location?"

"I was wondering how they could hide this from their ancestors, if this was real, I mean, there would be a historical place, but they dig it in a story book."

"What is on your mind?"

"This is apocryphal. I think this place is hidden as well, they never returned, they don't know about it, we must find a place that is not mentioned, a dig basically."

"You make no sense; do you want to excavate something?"

"Maybe. I need to know how the dragons lay their eggs, how they could get to that shore."

"You think that this is the bubble matter, matters?"

"The owl never said. Let's go to the Owl Dirndl and find out."

"Is there a place in these islands which is forbidden?"

The Owl Dirndl and Arethusa looked astonished hearing Kurtz's question. The five men and the two owls gathered around a table with open books.

"Forbidden? We are owls for god's sake, what could we hide or forbid?"

"You just have to say, don't fly there...." Fife started, but Kurtz interrupted.

"They are owls, they can see everything, even the spiders."

"Spiders, what spiders?" asked Four.

"I don't know what you could think of.., and why?" Arethusa asked Kurtz.

"So are there places where you do not often fly?"

"Like what?"

"Some place near the seashore, what you might have not noticed."

"Are you asking this, does this have anything to do with the bubble matters?"

"Well, yes, if I knew what the bubble matters are, I could tell you."

"Oh my, you haven't been told..., I say..., So we have been experiencing certain phenomena. It started right after you left the holy land. There have been these bubbles that come from the sea, bluish in color, most energized."

"Energized?"

"Well, yes, they glow even when the sun is up. They are the flesh of dragons."

"You think they are dragon eggs hatched?"

"Well, we know this... for sure. When we had to face the first unlucky creature visiting town," said he in a sarcastic tone, "Well, we had to kill it and then investigate the whole matter."

"So how many?"

"Well, it is still going on, my friend."

"Where?"

"By the sea."

Fife looked at Kurtz, sighing. Half-Tongue entered the room from a door hiding in the darker corner of the room.

"You are awake," Arethusa said.

"Hello, Kurtz! How... I am so glad to see you... here," Half-Tongue ran to hug him.

"I am glad I have found you here," he said, hugging him back.

"You don't need those books anymore, I think," said Arethusa.

"What books?" asked Half-Tongue, confused.

Kurtz ignored him, asking back to Arethusa.

"So, these are the bubble matters? The dragon eggs. Is that why you brought him here?"

"Not fully, not unfortunately. We have other issues, but one has overwhelmed our minds lately so strongly, we have become more than desperate. They also look like bubbles. So, we concluded that this other phenomenon is related to the appearance of the dragon eggs."

"What, how? Where?"

"Well, we have to wait for that. It is only visible after dusk."

"We have plenty of time until then, four more hours... I suggest tea with milk and freshly baked sponge," hawked the Owl Dirndl.

"I am in," said Half-Tongue, thirsty and exhausted from the recent commotion in his life, "and I insist that you explain everything. What I have asked you recently, what you have not told me, what you were not to tell me and what you are not meant to tell me. Everything." He was desperately angry about what was happening to him, and he wanted Arethusa to feel this.

"Well, yes," hawked the two Owls, almost at the same time. "We will tell you... the time given; you have to know everything."

"Where, where... Where could we have space for all this... let's go to the library."

"This looks like a library to me... with all these books," said Four.

"Well, it is, and a small one," said Arethusa, "The real library, well, as you know, they are always hidden. This door leads underground to another underdoor. Please, make your way downstairs, I am going to create a Victoria sponge for you."

"Three," said Four, "I have not eaten cake for years..."

"How come?" The Owl Dirndl looked at Kurtz inquiringly.

"Well, Earth, and the Vertical complex... it is not what it used to be. We don't have food. Not cakes."

"A sponge is such a simple thing, my dear..." the owl was curious, "What happened?"

"We became too many."

"Your species? Too many people?"

"Yes, and disasters. And so many things... if we have time later, I am going to tell you everything," said Mof, watching their conversation silently from a corner.

The owl turned to him and said, "My old friend... the tired one... please all of you, gather in the library and wait for me."

"Hm." Kurtz murmured, "This looks like some kind of a hive structure. Strange enough, though."

"So, you see, as I told you. We have never seen anything like this before in the sky. The sky in our world," and the Owl scratched his head, "Well, this is not what you would normally expect from a sky because of the variance in physics and elements, but even calculating that in and magic, we have not come, we could not come to any conclusion why this thing has appeared on our horizon."

"Well, strange enough," Kurtz lowered his head to his shoulder. His eyebrows were moving up and down slowly. The others know this expression on his face already, the faint recognition, the slow awakening.

"Kurtz, what do you suspect?" Thee asked him, reacting to his face.

"Yeah, I might..."

"What" hawked the Owls, "What do you know?!"

"Well, I don't know. I can only guess but let me see this phenomenon first. Do we have a looking glass?"

"I don't have one. But if you like I can describe to you what I see with my eyes."

Kurtz raised his arms to form a looking glass with his hands, which gave him a sharper look of the area he was watching.

"No thank you, I can see. I wonder how far this thing can be. Have you measured?"

"Measured? What? The size?"

"No, the distance. How far is this structure?"

"Well, we have not... tried to measure the distance," the two Owls looked at each other embarrassed, "I would not have any idea, why?"

"Well, we may be able to identify its source. I am not sure it is not moving."

"Moving?!"

"Well, it looks as if it was growing, so I am guessing it is moving or coming closer at least."

"How could we measure it?"

"The distance? I have an idea. I will perform magic," he laughed at the two Owls and pulled a small book out of his pocket.

"It is the stomachion?!"

"Yes, and if my memory serves me right, Archimedes had this ingenious machine to measure distance. The ODOMEETEER." He said this last word slowly and loudly.

"The odometer?"

"Hell, yes," said Mof, "I remember that machine," and he looked at Fife.

"It is in *De Architectura*," confirmed Fife.

"THE WHAT?" cried Half-Tongue out, left floundering by the mere mention of any further books.

"*De Architectura*," repeated Fife himself, sighing, "I am sorry, Half-Tongue. It is a book written by a Roman military engineer."

"So what?"

"Well, it is a machine that can measure distance."

"In space??"

"Well, it is some kind of structure. With wheels. The number of turns..."

"Will give the distance, I see," interrupted Half-Tongue.

"But... I will perform magic," Kurtz blinked an eye.

"So, how do you do it?"

"Do what?" Kurtz asked.

"How do you perform magic?" asked Half Tongue, "and I saw them doing it already, the owls can also do it."

"It is not what you think. It is what you do not think, rather. Simply physics, in a different universe. Which this is not. Same universe, I mean. All about overactive bosons and different levels of energy. You are magic for lice. They will never understand how you can do it."

"Oh, but how would it work in practice? Like the magic wands?"

"Rather a lot of thinking, I say. And something I saw two hundred years ago."

"Two hundred? You are not more than forty, Kurtz," he pressed his name with a little astonishment.

"I was born in 1926."

Half-Tongue turned away from him and looked at Fife.

"I... after all what happened... I don't know what to say..."

"What will you say to me? I am 2100 years old. And Mof? He is 6053."

Mof looked at him with an odd light in his eyes.

"I don't know my age. I was born a very long time ago, in Asia, and..."

"What? But how could that be... Is this somehow connected to where we are?"

"Not really, it is just another place in time. I mean in our time."

"In our time. Do they have other times?"

"Well, I have proof that other times exist."

"Waaait, waaaait, waaaait, I'll tell you the whole story," Fife interrupted Kurtz.

"There is a spot of light, a photon, that arrived to Earth a long time ago, before humans could have existed. It escaped from another world; it is an escaped photon. It is a different one that we have in our world. It has shorter wavelength for the color of light than expected, it has greater energy. We measured the speed of oscillation, and we came up with 186,287 miles per second. It is 5 miles more than the speed of light in our universe."

"So here is this oscillating thing, whatever you call it..." Thee shook his head from the effort he needed to explain. "It stopped there, we do not know why. It has the frequency to travel through material."

"Well," Kurtz seemed to have a lot more to say about the nature of the oscillation, "We know why."

"So why has it stopped?"

"Yes... the earth has the exact magnetic frequency that blocks or absorbs its capability to travel further in material. It is trapped in that place."

"Is it not absorbed?"

"No, it hangs there, trapped."

"Where?"

"In the sea, where we came from... Well, we were not born there but each of us met the light under the sea, in the water."

"The Escence," added Thee.

"Escence."

"We call it Escence because it did not match any other luminous color. Not fluorescence, not incandescence, nothing."

"What does this have to do with magic?"

"Probably a lot. I mean for us it means we are capable of doing things. And we dont die."

"And what about the Wind lords? Who are they?"

"Well, that's us."

"We are the Wind lords of Escence," Four laughed at Half-Tongue, "Yeah, that," Kurtz smiled mockingly at him.

"So how would it work in practice?" Half-Tongue asked. Kurtz gave him a sceptical smile, but Half-Tongue was still looking back at him, wriggling with curiosity.

"All magic is metaphorical."

"YOU ARE secretive," answered Half-Tongue.

"Even for me, it is still a big puzzle, somehow."

"The stomachion?"

"Hell, yeah. You two were talking," he shot an inquiring look at Arethusa, "So, it works like a metaphor. I want to raise the wind, I think of it, flap my coat and I'll reap the whirlwind. Like a caveman for rain."

"Oh."

"That's the basics. But I'll give you another example. I will mark protons to build this enormous device."

"The odometer?"

"Yes. So, I mark protons. I'll tell you step by step. You can't see it because the protons are far-far away from each other. The device is basically invisible, I would say it does not really exist, it is a simulation, rather."

"Oh."

"A creation of my mind," Kurtz continued, "projected onto the particle field. So, these signed protons, will make up this machine, will travel a distance to that hive for me on subatomic level. Information and energy, all there is to it. So, the protons will bring me back a distance," he stopped for a second, " A DISTANCE OF 20000 MILES?" he almost shouted the number into Half-Tongue ears, whistling with surprise.

"So it has returned?" Half-Tongue looked up to the sky, plucking his finger on a ray of light from the cells of the hive.

"Yes," said Kurtz, "It has returned."

"This seems to be an overwhelming structure. But not very close," Kurtz scratched his head, "Have you gone out there? I mean, now we know it is as far as the upper atmosphere, so have you flown around to see if it is, I mean if this is everywhere?" Kurtz uttered anxiously.

"Yes, we did receive reports, it seems to be all pervasive... everywhere you fly... you can't see the end."

"So, your planet is in the middle of this structure, I presume... what I need to ask you, if you have observed any changes... in your everyday life... I mean in physics or something..."

"You mean?"

"Changes you can't account for, now I know you have almost perfectly sharp sight, so do you experience anything unusual?"

"Now you say it... when I bake a cake- you know, it just does rise a little higher, though I have set everything to that level of perfection, expecting the cake to be perfectly smooth and straight. And now, since this thing has appeared- we have issues."

"But something more outstanding?"

"Well, no, as I said only this small detail, but as we all know, the devil is in the details," he hawked curiously.

"The devil is in the details," Kurtz repeated, murmuring. He turned to Fife.

"I've been thinking. About the shapes of these bubbles."

"Yes?"

"I have seen them somewhere before..."

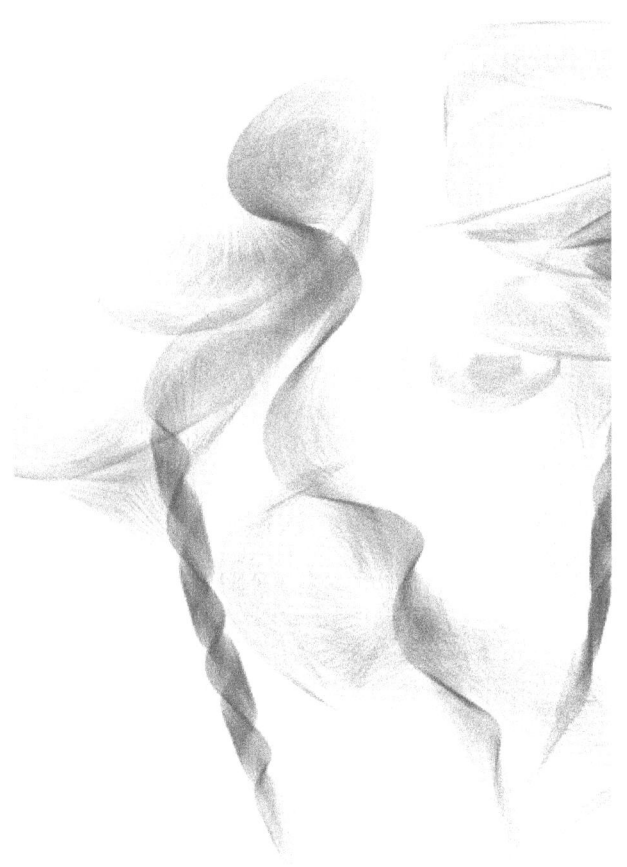

The warriors were two or three inches tall, very slim, they looked like small knots in their bubbles. The bigger the bubble was, the bigger the warrior could grow and unfold in the air after birth. They were writhing in hungry eagerness. Their bodies were fluid, but never evaporated in the sun. Half-Tongue and Arethusa were standing by the sea on the rocks.

"They are coming up," whispered Half-Tongue, "But why are they moving in a spiral..."

"It is the mechanics. The screw."

"Hm?" Half-tongue looked at him embarrassed.

"This magic was built on the mechanics of Archimedes' invention," he pulled a small book from his wings, "This was in the Stomachion I gave you..."

He pointed at a small drawing in the book.

"This device was designed by Archimedes to bring water up from a mine. Here they use it to that certain effect. It is again the mechanical principle that governs the magic, I should say."

The Wind lords were standing not far from the crushing waves, looking at owls who were capturing the small bubbles.

"Are you going to eat them?" Four asked an owl standing by his side.

"HMMM. That would upset my stomach," said the owl.

Kurtz leaned to Four's left ear.

"The mosaic floors. Did you see the mosaic floor? It looks like... these are very similar to that," he whispered.

"So, what happens to these creatures?" asked Half-Tongue.

"After this phase, we desiccate the bubbles. They will die without that liquid."

"Most human solution," said Thee, looking at Arethusa. He could not resist the pun.

"Well, after that..." Arethusa sighed, "We build them into our houses. You could see them in the Owl Dirndl's house."

"Arethusa," said Kurtz, "and Half-Tongue... I would like to travel to a place with my friends to look into this bubble matter. I mean the other one, that hive. We will come back soon. I will take you home when we get back," said he, blinking at Half-Tongue.

Part 7

Gypsy samurai

The fog in the sky

The sky above the skyscraper was a color of blue. In a hive of whiteness, the sun was pulsing to an unfamiliar rhythm.

Masura decided to enter the building. These buildings held the remnants of the human past, belonging only to his people; to those he knew. He collected things that were buried in these buildings, small and big fragments from the sunken era of electricity. The buildings had stopped working gradually, but those that kept up the longest, often had special generators. You could tell by the sheer state of the building if there was one inside; the only thing still working using electric currents: generators. They were big fish on the market.

He spat in the rain. His girlfriend could not stand his spitting. Masura was a well-read boy, who read and collected books – but was not of sophisticated origin as his girlfriend was. She was of high expectations, and Masura often thought that she would leave him soon. Not as if he was not a big fish himself, as he was clever and often showed up as a talented collector of the old things.

He also wrote poetry. Unwanted words, fine words, in unwanted order. A faint memory of ecstasy in his veins and genes. When he put his pen on a paper or wrote into a book because he had no paper, new senses arose, new feelings erected, to take him on a journey to a sparkling new world.

It was never the same; he never wrote what he had in his mind, but to experience the new. A trance far from his motionless world, which was fainting on the energy of hidden petrol stations.

He entered the building. The doors of the forsaken buildings were often open, people hardly ever closed the gates when they left them. It was not uncommon to leave doors and gates open in those years; you could never know when an outage would hit the hapless building. When the generators went off, people became hysterical, and generators often could go off. Now they served at the plantations to produce food. Animals were not as sensitive as life had been back then.

All was silent now. Exhaustedly silent. You could not hear the rain here. Going up the stairs, he had to realize his bag was already heavy for new things, so he decided to sort the bag out. The building seemed to be untouched; he had high hopes for his special favorites, the syringe, which was white crow – very rare; you only found them in special aid places, bathrooms, or restrooms. Searching was not simple when you were in a building adding up to six hundred thousand square meters. Drawers, boxes, bags. Thousands of them. You had to know the old logic of the drawers, finding out how those people worked and lived here. What they kept in the metallic ones and what in the desks. Sometimes you could tell it by the smell of the content. Often Masura became embarrassed with the metallic ones: they could be very personal. Obviously, the aid rooms were his hit places, but his interest in the drawers often paid him with curiosities, just as well as success.

He also collected things his people did not really need. Unwanted books were frequently in his bag, even now. He often revisited the buildings, where he sometimes had left the books in a hidden bundle. He chose metallic drawers to hide them, even if there was a fire in the building, the books were safe. He sorted out his bag and found a good place for the books. He looked around so that he would remember everything well when he would have to find it.

He did not notice the cracked crow creeping into his bag.

Masura put his skates on and started to roll towards the meeting place. He had been rolling for long when he noticed crows were following him. You had to fear the crows. Always En-Masse. They ate you. If you were moving. He stopped and gazed into the eye of the crow-mass, this iron cloud of oblivion. They were circling around him, and they were all insane as was the sky above.

He was waiting there among the crows in the rain, which had been spitting incessantly for thirty-two years. They said it was not like this before, but no one knew why the raindrops had to fall from the sky all the time. The color of the sky was almost always blue, never white from the clouds. There were no clouds in the sky, only that net of whiteness dimming through. Sometimes, especially in the early and late hours of the day, the sky was light grayish or almost white. *The fog in the skies* was their name for it. No one knew what had happened to the physics of the earth.

He waited for the crows to leave. The mass left him in the middle of the road on his fatigued hunkers. He was weather-beaten, his body worn out; nevertheless, his mind answered the impulses from the outer world without delay and solicitude. He started to roll towards his home.

"What can you find out there that is good for us and good for you? What are the best things you can find? What is it we need? How will you find a generator? What will you take home tomorrow? How will we survive tomorrow without you? What do you need in your home?" Signs swarmed the market from the windows of the merchant shops. It was an era of questions: they wanted you to think; questions were rational. The market was never too busy, so you could easily find anyone anytime if you were to meet there. His girlfriend did not come.

She was the only thing he suffered from, the only thing that could pervade the stability of his *equilibrium*. Their name for existence: *equilibrium*, a state of the mind, balanced, steady and rooted in curiosity. He started to cry.

Dres was coming towards him and, as he hardly could see anyone ever crying, he almost passed him with a faint feeling of astonishment. Crying was not unknown to them, but the equilibrium ensured their stability and weighed out the effects of small food portions, malnutrition, and depression. Dres looked at him in silence, frowning heavily, but his shadowed eyes got no answer. Masura gestured a farewell half-blinded and escaped to his quarters.

"I would not ever want children with you." His girlfriend came to break up. His face jerked under the tears; he could not speak.

"I see marriage as a practical way of life. I admired you for your strength and stamina, but I have become disappointed in you. I had expectations you could not meet. You have changed... I think you are naïve. I do not want to choose my mate based on emotions."

They had been talking for an hour and he was tired.

"I do not understand. What are you saying? I feel empty without you."

"We are really different."

He pulled into his bed to hide after she had left. His bag was left near the bed, and his jerking body woke the crow inside. He could not hear anything at first, but the animal grew more and more distressed, incarcerated in the heat of the bag. Its efforts to escape became more and more vigorous and louder every minute.

He forgot about crying when he realized the sounds were coming from his bag. He undid the knots, and the crow crept to the bed. Masura was out of his wits. A crow in his bed! His senses became overactive, and he had to sit down. He was staring anxiously at the crow. The crow sat up in the bed. Masura could see the cracked legs and the leaden blackness of the feathers. It seemed it was dying. His anxiety thickened; inching towards the ground very slowly, he crouched down low in front of the bed and the crow. Croaking. Then silence. Looking the crow in the eye made him curious. He crawled closer. It did not move, and he could touch it. His touch triggered the crow to jump forward. He landed on his back lying on the floor. The crow flipped a salto to his stomach and was poising there on his skin like some parrot on a swing. Masura made a blunt move to get rid of it, but he did not dare to touch it once more. The closeness of the bird paralysed him into a half-blind, half-deaf state of mind, his hands drooped powerless near his chest. The cracked crow licked his fingers. Masura grew callous. He touched the bird again, but now the bird did not react. He felt saliva accumulating in his mouth, thickly. He did not really know what to do. His eyes wetted and he started to talk to the crow.

"What shall I do to you? What...," he could not continue, the mysteriousness of human speech fired the crow into a painful attack on his face. He had to catch hold of the neck. The attack turned against his hands now, his blood was spilling on his clenched fists. He had to break the neck of the crow. It was lying on his stomach, his hands around the little dead body. He fainted. Thick saliva woke him. His mouth was full of it. He was trying to remember what happened to him, what made him lie on the floor. He felt the pressure of ten tons on his body, his consciousness answered him with delay. His girlfriend came to his mind and then the fight with the crow. He sat up and the body of the crow fell on the floor.

"This is insane...," his reason could not answer the confusion of painful emotions. He had to go away from this place.

He rolled to the building where he hid the books in the morning. He was rolling up the stairs to the top, rolling towards the closeness of the sky. He felt an urge to spit. Sweet saliva turned up from his throat.

He was hanging there, in the air, 1700 feet above the ground. He realized he was not falling at all, though he had fallen. He moved his hands and legs. It felt like jelly. He looked up and saw something very different in the sky than he was used to, the colors of the sky above the skyscraper whirled in patches of golds, whites and grays in a light tint of purple. Clouds, improbable clouds... and birds, strange new birds and things he could not make out. He tried to move laterally, back to the building. If he could climb back to the top, then go down to ground level....

He reached out for a piece of metal sticking out, and he could manage to flow closer. Trying to climb up to the top, he felt the wind stronger than before, the sound of the wind plugged his ears. Something cut him in the back. He turned around; spikes from a screech cleared his ears.

Part 8

Systems

"Hey! Look! Up there!" shouted Four, "What's happening?"

"It is not the cat or the mouse," Mof said, his eyes shrunken, looking up to the sky, into the white dimming light.

"In the air? That would be strange," Kurtz said.

"Why could they not be in the air? After all, they don't belong in this world," Thee looked at Kurtz.

"Well, they exist outside time and space, that's what we say, but..." Kurtz was thinking.

"It may be the bird," Thee said, sensing Kurtz's tiredness in his voice, "It's moving toward the building."

"Actually, it looks like a human. It seems to have limbs. It is struggling to get to the building!" Four looked at Kurtz in despair, "What's happening, Kurtz? What's happening to him?"

"I don't know. Let's go and see."

They entered the building through the open gates. The skyscraper was empty and felt eerily barren. They heard no sounds from inside at all, so they separated to look around.

"No lifts working. 120 floors," said Fife, returning to the lobby.

"120? No way."

"Hushhh," said Four, "I hear something."

"It is coming from that lift shaft. The sliding doors are open."

A sudden sharp clinking accompanied the arrival of Masura to their level. He was clinging crookedly to a thick metal wire with his bruised hands. There was a blunt banging sound on his touchdown.

"Who are you? Strangers," he asked when he recovered from his first surprise.

"Hey," they said, almost at the same time.

"Don't be afraid," Kurtz said, "What happened to you? Why don't these buildings go?"

Masura looked surprised upon hearing his question.

"Not one is going," he said, "most of the gens fell off. They don't work."

"The skyscrapers?"

"Yes. Where are you from?" Masura asked them.

"From here."

"There is some strange stuff up there, some kind of jelly. I was falling... I fell out of the building, but that stuff held me up... in some jelly... and that big bird came, but I could fight it off..."

"What bird?"

"I don't know. I have never seen a bird this big before!"

"What did it look like? Like an owl?"

"Hey skunk, I could not see. I was struggling."

"What is happening? Do you think they are owls?" Fife asked, turning to Kurtz, his voice fading away with every word.

"I don't know," Kurtz murmured.

"What is this planetary trauma?" Kurtz asked the people gathering around him in the marketplace, "This would be the secondary effect."

"Which was the primary one?" Dres asked.

"The sinking of the continent."

"I have heard of that," Masura said.

"What did you hear?"

"There was a continental collapse after terraforming. 300 years ago."

"300 years ago? How can that be?" Fife asked Kurtz astonished,

"This is still 2155, isn't it? Traveling never meant shifting time!

"Uh-huh," Kurtz murmured, turning toward Four who had just returned from going around the marketplace.

"Is this all you could find?" Kurtz asked him, disappointed.

"These could be useful."

"So where did you come from?" Dres asked Kurtz.

"France."

"France?" he asked with some hesitation in his voice.

"You don't know France?"

"I might have read about that. It must be far," Masura said.

"Can you travel at all? How can you travel?" Kurtz asked.

"We have the old petrol stations."

"You mean you use petrol? Is there petrol in the petrol stations?"

"Yeah, we have them almost full."

"How come you haven't used that?" asked Fife.

"We only use generators on the farms to produce energy. Transfers to kinetic. Nothing else works. Cars, yes, but we don't waste petrol on that."

"Cars?"

"Ah, some of them do. But we have experienced too many technical glitches lately, even with kinetic energy."

"It is strange that they are working at all. Do you know how long it has been raining?

"Thirty-two years. It's been spitting for thirty-two years. Never anything stronger. You can't even feel or see it, sometimes it is so delicate."

"So, do you know what happened? The second planetary trauma?" Kurtz asked Masura.

"What I know. We cannot do certain things humans could do earlier. Most things based on electricity don't work anymore. But we have the generators to work. They have this special insulation. Irandaam. This somehow protects the flow of electricity inside."

"Who built those generators?"

Masura shrugged.

"Do you want to see one? There is one at the back. It filters water."

"A filtering machine? How does that work?"

"It is all kinetic," Masura answered.

"That is strange that you are asking," Dres added, raising his head after a few moments of thinking while they were talking, "Because most of the generators that still work have the same company signs. Something like S. N. Sys Industries, or like that."

"The same company," Masura said.

Kurtz murmured a "that would not be strange", looking at Four.

"You know something?"

"Well, that is why we came here, because I suspected something like this. But the time shift... it just does not add up."

"How many people do you know about? I mean, how many people are there left on Earth?" Kurtz asked.

"Yeah, that's something we don't know."

"I could give you a raw estimate. If we can reach a satellite on course."

Four looked at him curiously.

"Do you think that there are still satellites above, in orbit? Is not what we saw was the holy land, above, the owls? Is this earth?"

Kurtz did not answer his second question

"Well, I don't know. We could try and reach one."

"You have your equipment in the cave," Mof said.

"Yes, I have hidden it in the cave."

"But why travel all the way to France for the equipment? Just to know how many people are there?" Four whined, "Where are we anyway?"

"Well, that is not the only reason why we need that cave. I would need the equipment to measure. To see all this. The reason," Kurtz said laughing.

"So, we are traveling. Flicking?"

"I don't think so. We might shift in time again, from what we know. We need to take people with us. I will need people to lift."

"I will find people for you who can travel with us. Are you saying that you can solve this? With your equipment. In that cave?" Masura asked.

"We have to try," Kurtz said, looking at Masura thoughtfully.

"Hey, what's the matter? Why are you crying?" Masura glared down at his ex-girlfriend sitting on a rock inside the cave. They traveled with the others to the land that was called France in the old times, hoping for a better future.

"Hey, Masura... this whole thing is just so... what if they don't find the answer? What if they can't solve this? I am so...," she hid her face in her palms.

"Do you remember when you fired me for the last time? And you told me those things, about ambitions and children... I was crying in my bed after you left me, crying my lungs out... I had to...," Masura looked into her eyes. She felt ashamed.

"What happened?" she asked, sobbing.

"I had these very strong feelings in me... and this crow crawled out of my bag, and I killed it... 'cos I did not know what to do... and then I rolled back to that building too...," he lifted his hand to touch her face, "I did not know what to do... and then after the fall, and that bird attacked me..."

"Why did you fall?"

"Hey, I don't know. It's just that if I did not have those feelings... I don't know... I wanted to tell you about these things before, it is just... I don't know how to say this..."

"Say what?"

"You know all this, the equilibrium, and what you have said... your mind. I have always wanted to change your feelings for me, but you did not change and that was all right. But I have always felt that it was the equilibrium that you spoke for. And most often it is the things that we say, that will change everything. Change your mind. And not what is happening to you. What is happening to you destroys your feelings and the life in you... you only learn fear," he silenced for a second, "But me, I could live in those words..."

"You mean poetry?"

"Yes, and I could love in those words and survive in them. Just like now."

"In the end, when the world falls apart, it is words and feelings that save us," said Four contemplatively, hearing the conversation between Masura and the girl. They were sitting around a fire in the cave, finishing their breakfast.

"Only words and feelings to live by," added Kurtz, "How strange this kid could grasp the feeling I wanted to say."

"Hell, yeah, you could build an empire on hatred from scratch," said Fife.

"Why would you want to do that?" Four looked at him blankly.

"The kid is a poet, you heard," said Fife, looking at Kurtz, and turned to Four, because he was still staring at him questioningly.

"I was born in Rome, boy," he said.

Kurtz looked at Four, he could not pocket his smile.

"Rome was an interesting empire. Life was almost always never about love. The empire of sombre days," Kurtz smirked.

"Uhuh," Four was yawning.

"Couldn't we build something like a Faraday cage?" Thee said, returning the conversation to the technical issues.

"How big?" Fife smirked.

"Oh, I didn't mean a cage around the planet, after all we don't even know what produces this field or whatever...," Thee was thinking.

"But some kind of insulation like the generators have?" asked Fife back," That's 50 kg per square meter. How do you build it around a wire? Extreme load of metal for a single wire."

"What about counter-flow wiring?"

"How would it solve the cancellation? It cancels everything. Even the generators are affected by now, behind tonnes of insulation."

"We found things in the back," Dres and his friends returned from an early morning exploration. They could not sleep late, too anxious to find a solution.

"It's scattered all around. What could have happened?" Fife asked Kurtz, waiting for the others to collect small and large equipment.

"Probably some animal. These still work," he had switched on everything he had close by, "These were all manufactured by the same company."

"S.N. Systems Industries," Fife read.

"Date of manufacture?"

"2022. 2015. 2009. 1997," whistled Fife, "This goes back way too far! Why?"

Kurtz did not answer immediately.

"Did they know this all along? That something like this will happen?"

"Remember when I joined you, back then, in 1978?"

"We remember," Mof said, "There was a lot of commotion around the place after that."

"They used that light for their experiments."

"The CIA?"

"Yes. But this was not supposed to happen, I don't even know what happened. They realized that the presence of Escence affects the flow of electricity in the wires and the equipment. They developed this insulation."

"That's why they could not use the bitgun on you? Not the satellites, nor the bitguns."

"Not those ancient ones, no. So, they put the full experiment on satellites."

"And what happened?"

"I don't know," Kurtz said, "This shifting in time means something... somehow the worlds have become connected. It is like some quantum superposition, like what we could see in the space jumps. A special moment."

"This special moment," said Fife sarcastically, "that took two hundred years to happen."

"We are close to the solution," Kurtz murmured, "We have to know better than this," he looked at Fife, his eyes raised in supplication, "I think it is the quantum oscillation to cause this shift in time. They were supposed to compensate for that, but it seems to have stopped working."

"What should we do?"

"Let's see the equipment first," Kurtz said, making his way inside the cave.

"We have to know better than this," Four murmured to himself.

"Better? How is this going to be better?" Mof yawned, "I've seen the future in every century since mankind woke to conscience, for a long, long time... It never got better."

"Are you two talking about the future?" Kurtz asked Mof, looking back at him.

"How, do you think, Kurtz, we can change this? I just think that all this is too much for us... but I can't accept the way we are either."

"We can't see out from the cave to the future," Fife was laughing.

"It was always like that, the same for us. The future is not outside," said Kurtz, "It's in the depths of this cave."

Future?

"Ah, you are awake," hooted the Owl Dirndl, seeing Half-Tongue coming through the door to his library.

"I was not sleeping well. What is happening? With all this waiting... I am starting to become impatient," Half-Tongue said.

"Sooooo what has happened? You know Kurtz, he was working for your secret organization, CIA, when he fell into the water. He is one of the Wind lords, who you know by the name Kurtz," said the Owl Dirndl.

"The old man from the forest?" Half-Tongue asked.

"Yes."

"He was aware of that photon, stranded in your world, and later he went back to that place with equipment," the owl pulled his head above a cup of tea.

"So, what happened?"

"They, I mean the CIA were experimenting with the oscillation frequency of the photon, but not on earth, which would have been too risky... but they were using satellites in space... in orbit around the earth..."

"Yes?"

"They used that same frequency to recreate the same effect around the photon. They, obviously, were not able to move it. And they connected more satellites, which, I do not think they noticed at that time..., created a full circle, a self-feeding oscillating circle around the globe."

"Uhuh," said Half-Tongue sceptically.

"They did not know about the deeper stringing of our worlds or anything about how this self-feeding photon circle would affect their world. It is our quantum physics as well that is affected and that of the earth," the owl stopped for a while, "this collapse, of my world, into your world is a superposition of the quantum particles. Your world both here and there."

"So, has it stopped? And what about that bubble machine?"

"Ah, that. That is not a machine."

"I am mixing it with the odometer. So what?"

"It's a photon phenomenon caused by that same quantum accident. In the upper layer of the atmosphere. Our fate is construed by random subatomic events that may or may not occur," he said with a certain darkness in his voice.

"This whole story... everything, how they intertwined, it is too complicated. I can't find a way to understand it or see what is true."

"You don't believe it," the owl said smiling.

"I find it hard to believe it."

"Kurtz likes to talk about the truth."

"Yeah, I know him. Is he here?"

"Not yet," he silenced for a while and then said, "Truth has uncountable faces. It will never be ultimate, as it can never be, but it always led him to do something better. I understand science, but I have never believed it to be definitive or ultimate... many will fall into that."

"How could I go home?"

"Home?", the owl scratched his head, "now that the overlord found his particle, and destroyed the satellites... the physics of the earth is going to recover. But you need to wait, more time than you think. Time has changed...," the owl slanted his head toward him, "Time has been damaged."

www.ingramcontent.com/pod-product-compliance
Lightning Source LLC
Chambersburg PA
CBHW051213170526
45166CB00005B/1880